Cinematic Lessons From
Abbas Kiarostami

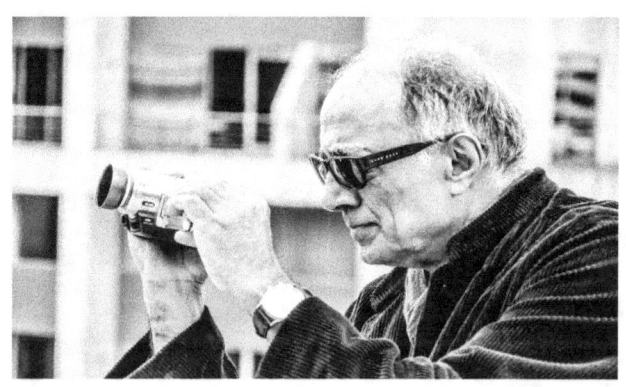

Cinematic Lessons From
Abbas Kiarostami

Mahmoud Reza Sani

Foreword by Jean-Claude Carrière

© 2013 Mahmoud Reza Sani

2st Print Edition (English)

All Rights Reserved. Except as permitted under the U.S. Copyright Act of 1976, no part of this publication may be reproduced, distributed, or transmitted in any form or by any means, or stored in a database or retrieval system without the prior written
permission of the copyright holders and publisher.

Published by: IMOFIS
INTERNATIONAL MOVING FILM SCHOOL
 http://www.imofis.com
info@imofis.com

Translation by: Alireza Lalehfar

Cover Design by: Azadeh Jahantabi Nejad
Foreword Translation, Editing & Formatting by:
Melanie Hughes Photos Courtesy of Lili Marsans except where otherwise noted

Translation by: Alireza Lalehfar
Cover Design by: Azadeh Jahantabi Nejad
Foreword Translation, Editing & Formatting by:
Melanie Hughes
Photos Courtesy of Lili Marsans except where otherwise noted.

ISBN-13: 978-1725896291
ISBN-10: 172589629X

International Moving Film School

*Tis book is dedicated to
my wonderful parents,
    my friends who believed in me
and the dreamers
    who have a story to tell.*

Contents

Acknowledgment	
Foreword	
Introduction	1
Art makes you Think	3
Gaining Experience is the Best Part of Cinema	4
We Work Harder when We are Limited	5
Men at Work	6
The Basis is in the Differences	8
Are there Different Versions of Reality?	10
Reality Comes from our own Personal Reality	12
Reality Disappears when there is Control	14
We must Learn the Language of Communication	25
Beauty is Painful and Difficult to Endure Alone	27
Life cannot Go On without a Poem	29
Open Your Third Eye	31
Cinema means Revisiting Childhood	34
We Express our Objectives through the Picture	35
Trust only What you See	37
Use Sound to Improve your Work	40
Our Duty in Cinema is to Delete Unnecessary Elements	43
The First and Most Important Viewer of Your Film is Yourself	48
Try to Talk Edited	50
The World is Work and God is the Worker	54
Film Always Starts without an Opening	58
Have Self-Confidence	60
Directing an Actor's Performance	68
Nothing Helps you Work more than Deletion and Selection	71
The Ending of your Film must Give Something More than the Rest	75
We must Shorten Everything for Better Communication	77
Be Aware of the Story	80
You Shouldn't hurt the Viewer's Beliefs	83
The Picture Separates Itself from Literature	86

Stories are Everywhere if You Look Hard Enough	89
My Father Killed Himself with Work	91
You must Turn your Knowledge to Personal Knowledge	94
Video Art: Turning Fantasy into Reality	96
I am Still Looking for a Walking Stick	99
Sometimes the Story is too Much	101
Cinema doesn't Need so much Strange	105
We shouldn't Impose Anything on Our Characters	108
If We want to Hear We must Learn to Be Silent	112
You Can give Story to a Documentary	115
Epilogue	122

About the Author

About Kiarostami

Acknowledgment

I'd like to thank the following people for their support, advice and help in making this book a reality.

Many thanks to my good friend Melanie Hughes for all her hard work editing, formatting, and more. Also the same to Consuelo Ramirez, Ahmad Natche and Ahmad Taheri for their hard work in the translation and correction of the Spanish version. Tank you to my publishers, Moein, in Iran, and Mohammed Sharif for his expertise and support.

I'd like to extend special regards to the writer, director, artiste Jean-Claude Carrière for his warm hospitality in Paris, his advice and the moving foreword he wrote for this book.

Lastly I would like to extend a big thank you to the master, Abbas Kiarostami, for allowing me a look into his world and letting me write this book. I will always be grateful for his patient mentoring and advice as I move forward in life.

Foreword

LESSONS OF REFUSAL

The lessons of cinema can only be given by a filmmaker who has never received them. Otherwise, he will only repeat the recommendations that he has collected from his masters, he will model his films after those movies and a film stuck in a sterile formula does not advance.

We see every day that American professors are repeating the old recipes and have never been able to write themselves a work worthy of emulation. It tramples the cinema, makes it stand still, which is the opposite of what we live. The same thing applies to literature, if we simply apply the poetic rules, for example we can write about our lives but never write a single poem.

By receiving the lessons of Kiarostami one must accept that we will never make the same movies as him. They refuse to be copied. Each of his films has a new part which belongs only to the director, who would immediately become banal if we imitate him. In other words, a film professor, if he is a filmmaker himself, can tell his students "how to," but he should never tell them "what to do."

What to do? That is for them to discover.

That said Abbas Kiarostami is the example, also a cineaste who using a very simple basis sometimes close to documentary, even a report, knew how to trace a personal journey which has surprised us for thirty years. He knows well the other work of what we call the great masters of cinema, but he did not imitate. At times it even feels as if he is trying to move away from them. In each of his films he gives the impression that he just discovered something.

What you should learn from his example, what to imitate, is precisely this rejection of any imitation. We must try to perceive, through the specific lessons he gives us, what is the force that helped him through all kinds of difficulties, to be able to renew his self constantly, with technical and limited financial resources. What we must take from him are these lessons of boldness but also the lessons of refusal and the first refusal to copy one's self. Do not constantly deepen your brow, achieve, reach, and surprise yourself, explore deeper, the more secrets, the more possibilities of expression: The true lesson is there. It is for us to receive, understand and use his example so that we can find ourselves and our individuality, that necessary singularity, which will speak to all.

Jean-Claude Carrière
May 12, 2013

Introduction

February 2012, Abbas Kiarostami traveled to Spain by the invitation of the Murcia Municipality Cultural Center to accept the Ibn-Arabi trophy for a lifetime of artistic achievements. At that time it was also decided that he would hold a 10 day filmmaker workshop for 35 students who had traveled to Murcia in eager anticipation to attend this once in a lifetime event.

I also traveled to Spain with Kiarostami, as part of the festival that was presenting him with the award and as part of the workshop. This book is the outcome of lessons we learned during that time. My duty here is to cite for those whom may not have the opportunity to attend this class and to summarize the days spent learning about cinema, for itself and for life.

Kiarostami believes that the major difference between his workshop and other schools is that the students start making films from scratch with no fear. Often cinema graduates don't have the courage to start making films because they tend to want to include all their knowledge into only one. They study for many years, have many screenplays ready, but they still keep looking for a producer with no luck and gradually become disappointed. In Kiarostami's classes the students start their work easily and smoothly and gain new experiences since no investments other than their time are involved. All of his workshops throughout the world are like that and most people leave these classes with one or two films, whereas prior to this workshop they might not have finished even one. The workshops usually last for 10 days and location is not limited to one student per film with several films often shot in a single location. More importantly people tend to find and make new friends during these workshops and build the groundwork for future cooperation. Students are able to work individually or in groups. This is often done individually by Kiarostami himself but he believes it is hard to deprive oneself from the joy of working with others, so he suggests not to work solely alone and encourages group participation.

The day after determining the subject matter, the class goes to see the preselected locations to look around and see the places in more detail. They then must find a story and describe it before Kiarostami and the others over the next few days so that their film does not become just another documentary. By doing this they are able to usually find both the positive and negative points and see the gaps in their stories. The master, Kiarostami, offers a constructive critique of their stories and then they begin to work.

"Our workshop project in Cecil was named "One Day Shooting" meaning we had to finish our shooting by the end of the day. Later on we had to change that because some students were particular and wanted to redo their weakest shots. So our screening was changed from one day to two or even three days shooting, but whatever it took, our films had to be finished by the last day. The only thing that mattered was that we must believe we could start and finish a film because each film is an experience in its own when time is limited and that's the important thing. I had a workshop at the London Film School nine years ago which was done with the help of TV channel 4. Each night a student's film was shown before the news and the broadcaster would say, 'The film you are going to see tomorrow night is not yet made.' The point was how we had to finish a project in a limited time and to see how pleasant these small experiences were and how much we could learn from them."

Art makes you Think

"Art doesn't make judgment, what art does is to make you think."
~Abbas Kiarostami

He was a painter at first before turning to cinema. He studied at a school of fine art, but he believes it is not important where you study or where you come from. As long as you know the notes by heart you can change your instrument any time. It is like exchanging your instrument with another one, which is not so hard.

"I studied at the school of fine art for 13 years. A four year period became 13 because I was a very bad student, mostly because my mind was ahead of my hand. I couldn't accept or recognize what I drew at all because I knew they were bad, and I believed my ability in painting had reached its limit and how much I had to work to reach the beginning. Then I started making advertisement clips, before that I drew and had a few books for children. Then I did some graphic work and made posters, credits and other things like this for movies. Later on as I came to know cinema, l was inspired. I knew I could go further in this art form than the others. But those first 13 years in school were very hard. Eventually the school gave me a bachelor's degree and set me free."

Gaining Experience is the Best Part of Cinema

He would not recognize himself as a professional filmmaker, and if it was otherwise he had no reason to start these classes and put in 10 days for it. After spending about 50 years in cinema, he has come to the conclusion that gaining experience by doing is the best part of this work. His highest goal in starting these workshops is simply for self-fulfillment and to experience new things along with others. He is also the type of filmmaker who will often make a few short films in between making features and even during his own workshops.

"Many people think the reason for making short films is to go and make big professional films later on, but it is not like that at all, at least it hasn't been for me. Short films encourage me and allow me to work on my next film with more confidence. It gives me courage so I don't think about the viewer or the producer or the investment so much. I didn't start these classes to teach anything to anyone because practically I cannot. I come here to experience anew the days when I was your age. That is the reason, otherwise I am not obliged to share my lifelong experiences with anyone."

We Work Harder when We are Limited

It is customary in his class for students to find and choose their story on their own within the theme of the workshop. The theme is usually based on a simple subject. Past experiences have proved to him that the students work harder when they are limited. Kiarostami believes a bit of freedom limits them and that a brought in subject frees them from those limits. So while they are limited on the subject they want, they are free to work within that subject.

"When we limit ourselves and stay in only one space to work, then stories come to you. It is like that prisoner who becomes a sculptor by working with dough because he knows he is limited inside four walls with no pencil, paper or anything else, his only option is to use the food they bring him, the dough. He starts working with it, not even knowing if he is going to make a sculpture. I think he makes a ball first. Then works with it little by little, gently kneading until it becomes a sculpture. This is the benefit of limitation. We have no producers here, our only luck here is that we have digital cameras. Sometimes students work with just a mobile in their hand. To me that makes no difference. I remember in school when we were given free subject matter for composition, no one could choose anything to write about and we used to tell our teacher that we didn't know what to write about. So when we are limited we go far and find stories within that confinement."

Men at Work

The day before class, we went to choose locations and decide on the workshop subject matter. We traveled about 150 kilometers passing through different cities and villages in and around Murcia. Kiarostami wanted to choose the subject matter according to the location and the people living there.

First he wanted to see the ocean, so we went to the shore but could not find a single person there. I thought an untamed location would help him choose a subject, so I took him to a desolate, deserted port with century old mines, but he did not like it and mentioned there was no one and the basis of our work is the people.

We then moved on to another shipping port, but there were only a few people there working with cranes to move the shipments.

Afterwards we went to a local beer factory. That was a nice place, in the factory the people had been replaced by robots due to new technology and now only a few engineers were left in the huge factory where so many people used to work. No one else was there but outside there was also a huge collection of orange trees stuck to each other and he thought we could make a story under the trees.

We went along with him and saw a few other places and a decision on the subject was made. The workshop theme was to be "Men at Work." The students would have to make their movies based on work environments. He thought the subject would leave their hands open since every moving, living thing could be a subject. Although students would be limited under the title "Men at Work," they were free to make whatever they want.

"I really do not believe that I or any other person can teach you cinema or say you can learn cinema in 10 days, but what happens in the 10 days here is that you will be able to express what you know and that is important. It doesn't matter at all if your movie comes out good or not, the important thing is that when it's done you will have learned by doing it and not just by Kiarostami's words. It is also enjoyable because you will work as yourself and not like any other person. One problem with cinema schools is that they turn everyone into good filmmakers, but that is based on the information available in cinema. This way we find our inner selves because there is no obligation toward anyone and we are not supposed to make a masterpiece. You should think of it this way and ask yourself what you have given to cinema previously and what you can give over the next 10 days. You will certainly get closer to cinema, to yourself and your tastes will become more apparent. It will not be theoretical anymore. You will start your cameras to see what you can see and then you will be tested by your own actions and say, 'I am born in limited time and limited location, just like a new born baby.'"

The Basis is in the Differences

"Who is familiar with editing?" Kiarostami asked. Most were. "Has anyone filmed before?" Most had. "Has anyone made a movie?" Almost all had. Then he continued and said, "It does not matter if you haven't made anything before. You can and will start making one in this class and since you are filming based on a story in your head, you will be able to edit it and shape it in your head before you begin shooting the film."

I truly saw how close Kiarostami's remarks were to reality during his workshop. Ahmad Taheri, Kiarostami's translator in Murcia who had never made a film before made one with his small camera. One day when we were visiting the students while making their movies, Kiarostami noticed that Marta, the manager of the Murcia Municipality Cultural Center, who helped plan this workshop with me, was interested in making a movie. He encouraged her and she took us to a cottage with a herd of sheep in the field. Kiarostami gave her a camera and told her to make a film about them. He stood by her, guiding her and thus Marta, like Ahmad, joined the circle of filmmakers. Kiarostami was very pleased with the final result and liked her movie a lot.

"The best film at the workshop in London Film School was made by a girl who had never done any movies before. Those who are experienced can succeed only by putting aside their experiences because we want to work with newer methods and find personal solutions. How interesting would it be if all your films

were the same? The basis is in the differences. That is why I say at some point in these classes you will find how to look at cinema differently, what your taste is and what you will look for. You will film what you like because filmmaking is really simple and it is not only what they teach at schools. It is done just by looking and experiencing. First thing is to know how to look and then try to direct that look. These techniques in my opinion can be learned only in four weeks and it is not anything complex."

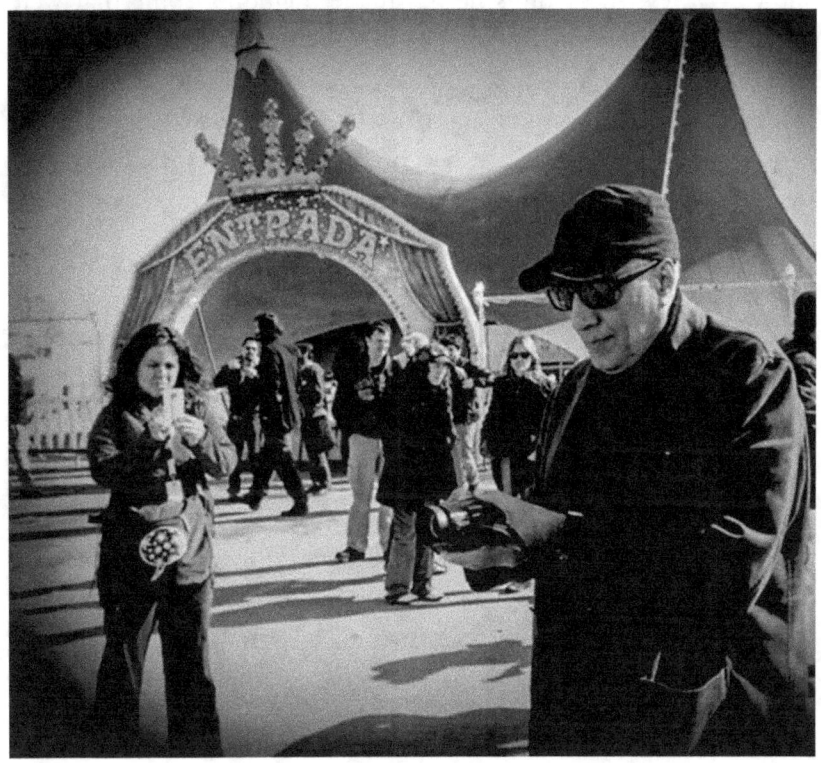

Abbas Kiarostami in front of the Italian Circus in Murcia, Spain.

Are there Different Versions of Reality?

The first day of class arrived. Kiarostami usually begins by showing a few short films he has made including some that were made in previous workshops. For this workshop he chose a movie called "Five" which included five short films. He also showed a 17 minute film called "Seagull Eggs" which he had made while staying at a friend's house near the beach. He was there for a week and decided to make some films about the sea and the subject of water.

"Seagull Eggs" began by showing some eggs trapped among a group of rocks on a beach. The waves were trying to steal the eggs with every splash. The whole thing seemed as if it was filmed in one shot. Those 17 minutes was centered around the sea trying to take and eat the eggs until it finally succeeded. Kiarostami calls for lights, turns to the students and says, "So simple and yet complex."

"How much can cameras tell the truth?" a student asked.

"What kind of question is that?" Kiarostami replied. "Why do we think we must tell the truth by camera? Can you feel the burden on your shoulders? If so, then why?"

"How far does the cinema that targets subjectiveness express reality?" The student asked again, changing her question.

Kiarostami was not convinced with the question and replied: "Please simplify your question, by simplify I mean talk about the film, your opinion, so I may answer your question through your opinion. Are you asking about this particular film or are you talking in general?"

The student, a young girl studying philosophy, named Clara, tries again to repeat her question more plainly: "This film is a true sample of objectiveness and you have taken it to reality as much as you could, right?"

Kiarostami: "It is not reality at all. Now that I put this movie on I realized it is not the real version, I have another version also. So how can it be reality when I have a few versions of this same film?"

A question entered my mind with Kiarostami's statement, "Are there different versions of reality?"

Reality Comes from our own Personal Reality

Students must show their own reality from the location, people and events they see. In his opinion we are not in reality since there is a separate reality for each one of us and so the reality is changed by our perception. Now the students must go to locations to see what they can do.

We went to see the locations for the workshop. On the way we arrived at a place where both sides of the road were lined with lemon and orange trees. Kiarostami was fascinated with their beauty and told me that many stories could be told there. "We must go and spend some time to see what we can get because graphically the place is bright, beautiful and full of stories. There can be two people under those trees or several workers, one could disappear, I don't know what could happen. Nice stories could come out of it, tragedies or even murder."

"Let's imagine we are prisoners in an orange garden and see what we can discover. Newton discovered gravity the same way, he was in a garden and an apple fell on the ground. We also have a beach and port with fishermen which Mahmoud and I are going to visit at three in the morning and I think good stories can happen there. Lots of people won't even consider going and sitting there, even for free. You have come from far away and we have come to play. It is true that this orange garden and the beach

belong to someone trying to make money from it, but we are going to take something else from it. Let's see what we will catch. Fishermen go to sea at three in the morning to catch fish, but when we go to the sea we will have something else in our net because fortunately or unfortunately we are not like other people; we look for something else. Let's go find it and continue our mental game. That's why we have nothing to do with reality; we will turn reality into something else, into our own personal reality."

"The sea you are looking at is real and everyone wants something different from it. As filmmakers, you have nothing to do with the real sea. You must give it new meaning. This is where art gets balanced with philosophy. Art and philosophy are not there so you can prove existence. They are here to breakup reality and express newer ones which are not forms, but norms, and playing these games are necessary to reach those norms; to say we will turn everything to anything and change the meaning of anything to something else. So once we say we are going to make a film about water, we should imagine what versions of water we might have. Naturally it gives life but as we saw in this movie it can also take away life. So as I say, if five or six of us sit under one tree or on one beach then we will have five or six different versions and stories. You can experience something that others have not if you do not then you have chosen the wrong profession. That fisherman takes a fish, weighs it and sells it to run his life, but when you go out there you must bring back something else. This is entirely personal and also entirely social. So if you are devoted to yourself and if you are not afraid of being exposed or to be open to reveal or disgrace yourself, (they laugh), then somewhere in this world there are people who will sympathize with you. This is where we don't choose our audience, they find you and only if you are original, if you don't lie, if what you say is part of reality for at least your day or your week."

Reality Disappears when there is Control

The movie "Seagull Eggs" was 17 minutes of one reality, however Kiarostami also had another version showing a whole other reality. In actuality it was two days, shooting six hours of film with the finished result having no basis in reality at all. Kiarostami and his friend bought the eggs from the market and set up the scene. The whole film was not taken in one shot as viewers imagined, but was almost 30 shots which were stitched together as one. Kiarostami had reality in his control.

"The sea would calm down every time a wave came and took an egg until it was hungry again then it would attack anew. The sea knew we had a camera there and it was doing it's work. So we have several realities but they are not in one form. You cannot just put the eggs there and wish them to be taken by the sea. They must be controlled. Therefore when something is in our control it cannot be reality anymore. That was my version of reality at that time and at that day and any movie you work on is the same. Any man moving in front of your camera is not in his own reality anymore, he is only part of reality. "Seagull Eggs" was filmed on two different days. One day when the sea was calm and wouldn't touch the eggs and another day when it took them all in less than a minute. It was hard moving down on the rocks and my assistant slipped many times. He put the eggs there and came up happily but when he turned and looked, the eggs were gone, taken by the waves. So he continued placing the eggs, we fixed the camera there and kept changing film. I think 10 cassettes were used. We then we edited these two days of film, putting them together, merging the calm sea with the uneasy sea. I could make this film as long as 90 minutes or I could leave the calm sea as long as I wanted to and say when the next wave would come to take the eggs. The whole film could also be edited into three minutes but then it wouldn't be so interesting because the drama was actually in the duration. The rhythm gave it meaning. The sea would calm down each time after it ate an egg, becoming full, then when it was hungry again it attacked and took another. This is where we interfere with reality. We change reality so we can dramatize another reality."

A young student from Brazil says: "The sound effect was like the birds were telling the story and they came to take away the eggs with excitement."

Kiarostami: "There were no birds and the eggs were goose eggs, not seagull eggs, because we couldn't find any. But who would want to know what kind of eggs they were any way? We colored them a bit orange and told our story with help of a sound effect, each time an egg was taken by the sea, a seagull cried out. We used sound effects and it became part of the story. Now many think we just put the camera there and everything happened at once. I asked a student once how the film was made? He replied, 'You were passing by and saw the eggs laying there, you fixed your camera and filmed it.' Then I asked him how would I know what might happen and why should I bother putting my camera there. You must know what you are going to take and don't put it on account of chance or luck and say 'I hope it will happen.'"

"Did you think there was a chance the sea would not take the eggs?" another student asked.

Kiarostami: "It had to, in fact as the creator, you must dictate how the sea acts, and the sea must come and take the eggs whenever you say. Of course you know you cannot mess with the sea because the sea will ask 'Who are you?' It might make a suggestion and say 'Look, take your shots on my calm days, and take your shots on my uneasy days, then go home and edit them.'"

Student: "I understand we should not leave things on chance. We write the script, plan the work and start, but when we see the condition up close should we try to change the conditions or should we change the script?"

Kiarostami: "Both of them, we must see which one is more powerful, us or them. If I really feel the other side is stronger, like this film you saw, then I say the sea is stronger than me, so you shouldn't fight with the sea and must think of a way to bring its wild nature under your control. On the other hand you may see the other side as being weaker and that's when you say I am more powerful and you think of a solution and ways to catch it the way you want. Now I ask you to watch a six minute film with me and I will tell you in which parts I gave in and which parts I made it give in."

We saw another film "Wood," one of the shorts featured in "Five." A piece of wood lies by the seashore, the waves comes in slowly up against the wood until it splits the wood in two pieces and then takes a piece with it. After seeing the film and also knowing the fact that we shouldn't leave everything on chance, the question came to mind, "How many hours had Kiarostami filmed before the wood broke and was taken away?" He told us that he placed a small amount of explosive inside the wood to blow it up.

"Otherwise you wouldn't go after such a subject because what would you do if the wood doesn't break by itself? How long do you want to wait? How should the wave take a piece and leave the rest behind? Well a piece of transparent string can be tied to it somewhere and can pull it. So half stays and half goes. But I am not serious about the string, (he laughs), we were just lucky for that one to go away. Sometimes luck helps and other times it doesn't. The part when the wood comes back toward us was done by itself, we only broke it."

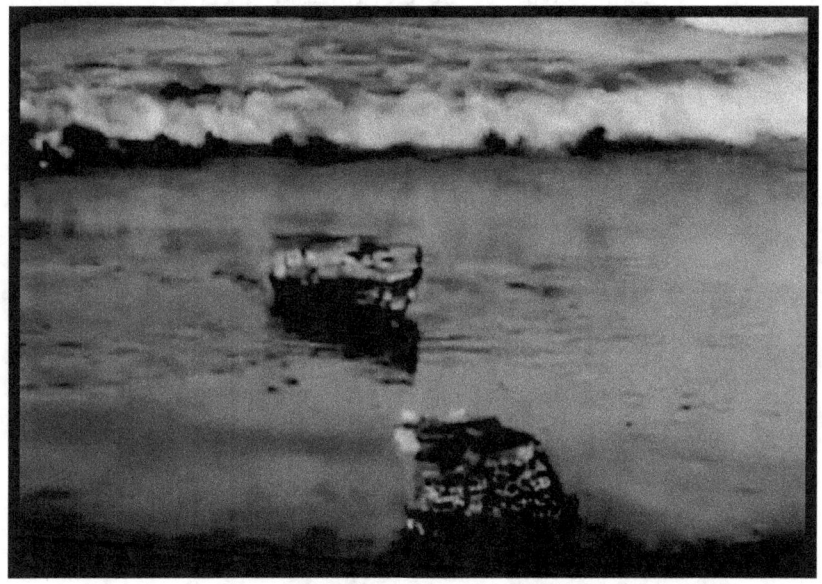

Still from the short film "Wood." Courtesy of Abbas Kiarostami.

Kiarostami changed the essence by blowing up the wood and by doing so reality expressed itself. He made something that he wanted to happen become reality.

We wanted to know if it was possible to do the same with people in movies. Could we change them the way we wanted to. Kiarostami said it is possible and he had done it before. In his movie "Where is the Friend's House" he arranged for the boy to take the notebook by mistake. The story was very real and the boy who was the main character didn't know what to do. Naturally a naive, country boy like himself believed anything he heard, Kiarostami told him they came from Tehran to give the notebook to its owner. At the same time their camera was running and this boy felt guilty the whole time he was being filmed. After a month of filming the boy finally told them he knew he was chosen to play in the movie and there is no real notebook involved. He used the same method in other films like "Close Up" and "Taste of Cherry." He believes under special conditions an environment can be created for even professional actors so they don't just act feelings according to the director's wishes. This method was clearly apparent in the movie "Through the Olive Trees." The whole time the lead actor was being played on and during filming he had managed to fall in love with the girl in reality. Thus he was able to create real scenes.

"In the movie "Taste of Cherry," a soldier gets in a Jeep, leaves with the lead actor and has a long conversation with him. I used to sit beside the lead actors but didn't give them the script to read. I just told them the story. He sat beside me as we drove up the hill which was on a curvy road. Nobody else was with us. I had the microphone turned on and the camera was fixed on the window with it's on/off key in my hand. So a regular team of filmmakers was not present and it was only two of us. We had to go to the top of the hill where I told him we were going to a job. He asked me, 'What kind of job?' I kept stalling but he kept asking. I made him suspicious of me by giving him displeasing looks. Then he asked, 'Where are you taking me?' I said, 'Don't ask,' (with an unfriendly voice). Time passed and then he said, 'Well, I should know what I am supposed to do.' I answered 'I told you, don't ask.' I then told him to open the dashboard and give me a piece of chocolate. But inside the dashboard was a knife. He saw the knife and said, 'There is no chocolate.' I said, 'OK, close the door.' He was completely nervous now, anxious to know where we were going and for what reason. You can see in the movie how real his feelings were. When we stopped the car, he really began to run up the hill (everyone laughs). I came up with a good idea of how to get rid of this guy. So during filming I told him to open the door, go out and run and watched him go. Then I put the camera on the other side and put the lead actor in my seat and fixed the whole thing during editing.

So now we have a question about how much do we have the right to push our performer, we will discuss this in more detail later on to see how far and with whom we can take this."

"I did the same thing with Mr. Homayoon Ershadi who played the lead in "Taste of Cherry." I asked my soundman to record my voice talking behind his back saying 'Well, unfortunately I have not made the right choice with him. He has a good face but no talent.' Then I had the soundman play the recording for him. That was simple enough to have him play the whole movie in a state of total depression; he felt useless. Of course he became a professional actor later on, but still he is not as good in any other movie as he was in "Taste of Cherry." This method is ordinary and doesn't belong solely to me. Fellini did the same thing which he wrote about in his memoirs. In a scene where his wife was playing the role of a prostitute, he yelled at her right in front of the crowd He did this in the street, in front of the whole camera crew. She had performed her best part in that movie because the tears were so real and natural. Naturally he hugged and kissed her later on with many apologies explaining that it was just a way to have her do her best acting. I think in the end that she was pleased too. This kind of play with others is normal in our regular lives too and others do it to us and later on we make up. If the outcome is good and gets on record then I too wouldn't mind being that piece of wood that gets blown up. I broke so many others, why not be broken, what would it hurt? Non-professional actors may not get the real feeling even though the director gives them dialog. The real feeling must be created, otherwise they just pretend. If there is going to be a sad scene the next day, the best way is to prepare their mind the night before. You should make them unhappy, so they sleep with sadness and the next morning they are ready and you don't have to explain how to get the feelings, all you do is ask them to say the dialog and leave the rest to them. If you want them to be happy then make them happy the night before. The best way for this is by indirect ways. I have worked with non-professionals for most of my career and my movie which I shot in Japan was no different. There was an 83 year old man who said he has been in cinema for 60 years but has never said a piece of dialog ever because he had always been an extra. Now you can't believe the dialog he had to say in this movie and how well he says it. Naturally I couldn't talk to him directly since I don't know Japanese, but I transferred my feelings indirectly to him through the translator and you see how great he played this role. He is like any big star, like the actors of American cinema in the '50s. That is because there is no single or simple formula for all. After you get to know someone then you know what to do with them so they give you the return what you want."

Student: "You said we must have control over everything, now what happens if we don't?"

Kiarostami: "What did you say you did before coming to my class?"

Student: "Mostly sculpture and photography."

Kiarostami: "What do you use for sculpture? What is your material."

Student: "Wood, paper, different things."

Kiarostami: "What do you use for photography?"

Student: "My camera."

Kiarostami: "Tell me what happens if you don't have control? For example if you don't set the shutter right?"

Student: "Sometimes I get more interesting results than I expected."

Kiarostami thinks a bit and says: "Well that's true. It is also the same for us, but definitely as a norm we must have control. Once in a while things happen that can't be controlled but you cannot leave it to happen by chance. We must control everything, and then let things show their true nature in that control. For example in my movie "Close Up" I couldn't control the actors blinking. I couldn't tell them when to blink. And sometimes they blink when you don't expect it at all and transfer feelings through it. Like a mixture of your control and their personality. There is a nice poem from Rumi which means that it is me who puts you in motion. I give you your first move, but then I have to follow. In fact I have to follow the path you choose. So I give the first swing but I become the follower."

Another student asks a question. "At the end of movie "Close Up" when the person is replaced by the filmmaker, a part of sound disconnects, was this actually a malfunction or did you do it on purpose?"

Kiarostami: "We did it on purpose. When the one character came to visit the fake, he was emotionally moved so much so that he forgot about the film. Hossien Sabzian, who pretended to be Makhmalbaf, completely forgot that we were making a movie. He got on the motorcycle and held his friend whom he thought he would never see again, but that scene had no real feeling at all. This was an opportunity for him to chant about cinema and society and other things, that's why he was not suitable for my film. The take was very bad and we could not re-shoot it. I kept thinking about what to do. You cannot believe how bitter that night was; he kept chanting and no one wanted to listen. So I thought we could do it like that and cut the sound then say the sound malfunctioned so no one would find out."

"Renoir, the painter, has a famous saying that he was painting once and at the last moment when he wanted to sign the painting some paint splashed on it from cleaning brush and ruined it. So what should he do? Should he throw it away? Then he thought he could turn it into a new element, he drew something with the smudge and turned it into a chair. But then he thought the chair is no good since the painting had a flaw; if that was a chair then a chair should have been there. So in many instances when things we don't like or didn't want happen, then think about finding ways to change it into something else in order to save to original. That is how we bring out something positive from something negative or bad."

Another student asks: "How do you correct phrasing or mimic problems while making your movies?"

Kiarostami: "It depends on the situation. Sometimes you cannot do anything and must throw it away. You cannot always make something good out of a bad thing. Some bad things have no capacity to become good and you must leave them, (they laugh), and if you are smart you won't waste time and accept that nothing good will come out of this one. If in fact it does have a good points in it then don't let it go, but tell me what exactly are you talking about?"

Student: "For example if an actor doesn't say his dialog correctly one day, how do you make him edgy on the same day?"

Kiarostami: "You cannot do anything if you haven't selected the right person. Basically the most important thing that guarantees your work is the right selection. It is important that you do your best to select the right people and then your job will be easier."

Student: "Have you ever gotten to the point where you tell your actors do this or don't do that?"

Kiarostami: "No, you cannot do that. The best acting comes when you don't make suggestions during the scene. Like a football coach, you have to do all your work before the game, know their abilities, and know how they will do. Put them in the right position and when the game begins you can sit back, watch and enjoy. I think directors who jump in the middle of the scene don't know their job. I believe a good director is the one whose job is finished when filming starts and just gives the cut at the end. It is wrong jumping in the middle and keep saying go left, go right, look up or look down. Of course there are times when it's OK to do that, like getting a close up of the face and say, 'Turn and look at the window,' but you cannot do such things in middle of an emotional scene."

"It all goes back to selection. My movie in Japan was the hardest movie I have ever done. It was so tough that sometimes I would wake up in middle of the night and wanted to pack my bags, run away to Iran and leave the film unfinished. The wish to run away made me feel better. It wasn't until later on that I found out why. I chose the wrong country and also I didn't select my group. They were given to me. One day someone walked in the door and said 'I am your camera man.' It was something like a shotgun wedding, (they laugh), then another came in and said 'I am your soundman.' And another one said 'I am your assistant.' When filming started I saw I couldn't make a connection with any of them. I was easy with the people in front of camera whom I chose but it wasn't like that with the ones behind the camera."

"So choosing the right elements for your work is very important and surprisingly signs of good or bad selection are there from the beginning. I don't know why sometimes we are so overconfident for no reason. Overconfident people are losers. If people are not what you want them to be, then there is nothing you can do. This is not limited to selecting performers, it's also true for our partners in real life too. Some people think they can change the bad manners of their partners, but they just put themselves and their partner through a rough time. It is best for all of us to think change is not possible, or if it is, it is too small to see in our lifetime. So in my opinion if we believe in change and want to change and keep our partner then we must make changes in ourselves. If they have remarkable characteristics then we must make that change within ourselves because you are more at your own service than them. The same goes for the movies. Most of the time if I see something I like in a performer, for example the face, I give them credit and I won't get rough if they get out of line once in a while. I let them do whatever they want and try to lead them to the place I want, but I let them take that path."

Kiarostami reminds the students again that the title of our workshop is "Men at Work" and when they leave they must think about the story and look at the people to find a scenario, basically saying anything that moves can be regarded as work and has a story behind it.

We must Learn the Language of Communication

For years Kiarostami has done more photography than anything else. He thinks communicating is hard work and it is difficult to deliver your points to others. Language is our only mean of communication but as he sees it, it is also a cause of misunderstandings. So we have to make it as simple as possible although at some point it will become useless and have no feedback. That's why I think photography satisfies him since he won't need anything else.

"I have been in photography for more than 30 years. I go out with a camera and take pictures. We have to learn the language of communication when it comes to working with others. This language is completely different than everyday conversation. It is a language that can get you closer to others and them to you, not create distances. How do you ask someone to do something for you? How do you say what you want and the hardest part is how do you know what you want in the first place? I think we obtain something first then decide if we want it or not. Our class here is one example, it is a solution for itself, it tells you make a movie to see what you can gain and then you may see if it is close to your needs or not. We have a poem that says, 'You plummet in path of love,' meaning you have to dive with your head, 'fallen blood at our feet,' ask nothing and make your move, 'the path alone leads the way,' when we don't know what we want we must make a move. When we take the steps, we gain, then we'll see if

it satisfies us or not. Isn't this what we wanted? Taking shots of something that you want is hard enough, yet harder if you don't know what you want. How many people in your life have you taken care of? Use this sentence to relieve yourself by saying, 'See, he doesn't know what he wants.' The number of people not knowing what they want is not small. This is some sort of... taking a shortcut. We obtain first then we see if we want it or not, because we don't know about our shots and don't know our needs. That's why I say we start to work in these classes very simply and with no expectation. We don't think about creating a masterpiece, we'll pick up our cameras tomorrow and make something. We wish for satisfaction and to find our way. We'll either say 'Yes, I like this work and I'll move on,' or 'No, I'll leave it,' and because we haven't invested anything, because we haven't given promises to anyone to make this film; we don't go around making a big fuss about it and we don't put the sponsor in jeopardy. We just make a movie and see what we can get."

Beauty is Painful and Difficult to Endure Alone

Every day we see a whole bunch of films being produced due to the high technology of this new era, but the question is why do we close their case in our mind right after seeing most of them? We just want to see the next one, until we go to bed agitated without being influenced by any of them or even left to mingle with a single scene in our mind. This, although, doesn't happen to me with Kiarostami's films and the pictures keep repeating themselves in my head. This also happened for most students attending Kiarostami's classes and they were curious to hear the reason from the master himself. We wanted to know his secret as to why his images stay and repeat themselves in viewer's minds long after they leave the theatre.

"Maybe the reason is that I don't make anything absolute. There are other reasons but maybe it is due to lack of definiteness and not presuming is one way of continuity. Another one is not making judgment. When you give final judgment for black or white, one guilty and the other worthy, naturally the story ends right there and that thing will not happen. There are many factors involved; I think it is important that we don't presume events happen, make no judgment and don't show it's black and white aspect. Expressing beauty without any interference makes you come across a phenomenon that no one has answered to but the beauty itself, because beauty is endless and no one knows the logic behind it. If one day you were fortunate enough to recognize a

phenomenon like that, you should know that it will stay with you forever. That might be the most important aspect, because there is an unfoldable secret in beauty and it will make your job easier and you may gain everything if you reach it. That's why they say beauty is painful and impossible to endure alone, that's why you like to share the beauty with others because you cannot keep it for yourself alone. This is the power of beauty that we cannot keep to ourselves. When we want to talk about a beautiful view, we keep repeating, 'I don't know how to describe it,' that is because we are unable to describe it. You want to share the beauty with others, such is it's power, but you just cannot."

Life cannot Go On without a Poem

Many say Kiarostami's cinema is a poetic cinema, but I say he is a poet who also makes movies. A poet in a new era who writes his poem with his camera. What is the relationship between his poems and his films? Poetry has been an intrinsic part of his generation. In the country where he lives life cannot go on without poetry. If you live in Iran, you see that it is impossible for someone of his age to end his day without reading a few poems, even those who cannot read recite poetry. Poetry was his window to the other world, not like today where the Internet is the gateway to our perception. He has always been more dedicated to poetry than most. He often spends his nights with poetry and has published four books of poems in the last few years.

I was reading his book of haiku poems recently and noticed how full of imagery they are and how each one could become a full feature or short on its own.

There is a short film of his that he often shows to the students. It ends with a picture of a dog burning. It is very emotional.

"*I read a haiku poem a long time ago that said 'All reports about Hiroshima were broadcast, they were all recorded, but yet no one reported anything about the butterfly wings burned in the distance.' This photo, the one of the dog burning was inspired by that. It was very painful. I burned my own photo. I burned 50 copies of that photo one by one until one burned just right because they wouldn't burn the way I wanted to. I wanted to give a little poke so we pay more attention to nature. The damage is not the subset of things being recorded somewhere. This dog didn't have a record, neither did the butterfly that burned in Hiroshima and no one knew."*

Everything begins with poetry for him. When I was reading his book of haiku poems, "Walking with the Wind," which contains around 350 poems, I thought to myself they all could turn into such everlasting movies in a genre that must be named Kiarostami's cinema. He is truly the king of this world he has created, a world that he can simply enjoy and return him to his childhood.

"On my will,

my childhood shoes

will be paired in front of me."

Open Your Third Eye

Cinema students always ask the same question. Should they prepare a script first and then go after location and other things or vice versa. Kiarostami cautions them that it can be done in many ways, but more importantly they should prepare themselves and clear their mind for what they are about to create.

"Open your third eye because every person who is disconnected with art and is doing something else has eyes too; the same two eyes you have. They can even live and run their life with only one eye, but you need something else and that is searching non-stop, looking. They look too but you must do more. Our mental status, that light bulb, must always be on and alert. We must find things that others passing by don't normally see. If your mind is clear you will definitely find things and notice your point of view is different from others. So we work with our films on the same basis, meaning when you read a newspaper you should read it differently than a businessman. When a businessman reads an article you can bet he only gets business ideas from it, even if he reads a novel, or a worker who plants onions sees an onion and thinks about this year's crop. So not only should you read differently, you've got to see the onion differently, this helps you find the subject. They say Hemingway once went to a gallery, he saw a painting of a landscape. There was a field with a cottage at the end with smoke coming out of its chimney. He calls the painter and asks how many people live in that cottage? Has their crop been good this year? How many girls and boys do they have? Are

the kids married? And so on… naturally the painter is listening to Hemingway astounded and confused. Well the thing is Hemingway was looking at the world from inside the cottage. There is no one there but he asks who lives there. What do they do? How many are they? How many girls and boys? So naturally our profession is the same. We must not be satisfied with the notion that the painter has done a good painting or not. We ought to be curious and see what is going on, subjects reveal themselves this way, through different ways. You are in a bus or subway and the person beside you asks for an address, you talk a little and all of the sudden you notice this itself can be a subject. For example the Koker films were a trilogy, the first was "Where is the Friend's House," the second "Life and Nothing More" and the third "Through the Olive Trees." In "Where is the Friend's House" I took the subject from outside of Koker, but the other two the subjects came out of Koker itself. The subject for "Close Up" was taken from a newspaper, the subject for "Taste of Cherry" was my own and the subject for my film that I shot in Japan, "Like someone in Love," came from a 17-18 year old girl dressed in white, whom I found out later on to be a prostitute. So you can find subjects anywhere if you look for it, in an elevator, a room or in a subway. We shouldn't skip; that light bulb in your head must always be on. That is something other people don't have and you must have it. So when you leave this place tonight to live your lives, you have to keep the third eye open to find the subject you are looking for. We have 10 days here and during this time you must experience making a film. If I were you I would keep repeating to myself 'Men at work.' Keep asking yourselves: 'Which workers? Where? What are they doing?' Then put your mind into whatever you feel like. We all know we have annoying thoughts and 10 days from now inevitably we go back to the same thoughts and we must resolve them, but during these 10 days we can put our mind to rest and not think about those other issues; just stick to the subject."

We went to see the locations the next day with Kiarostami and anyone who had an interesting subject or idea in mind would explain it for others in the bus. After some sharing, it was then decided that the students would continue and tell their stories and the films they were going to make the next day in class.

The only thing that Kiarostami kept asking everyone was to take it easy and not to expect too much or want to make a masterpiece, just to see what they can come up with per the space and the people. He emphasized this and that they had to limit their questions only to the theme "Men at Work."

Cinema means Revisiting Childhood

He said he was after the idea of childlike play in cinema, like those childhood games we played in our youth. One day he asked for a student's name. His name was David. Kiarostami told him that his name was something else to him and David is only good for his birth certificate. He said he has been changing people's names for himself for more than forty years now. He has been changing their homes, their jobs, their nationalities and imposing his stories on them.

"Our job is to play and that means revisiting our childhood, but not just to play, but rather to see who can David be? That's more important than who Davis is, that's exactly our job, that's what we do. There is a story about Kierkegaard in his youth when he was asked to write a composition about 'What do you want to do when you grow up?' In order to help him they told him to go out and look at different jobs and see which one you like. Kierkegaard was 10 years old then and says that he went out and saw a motorman, another salesman etc. I saw lots of jobs too but didn't like any of them. Instead I wanted to change their jobs because the motorman looked more like a teacher and I wanted to put my own teacher in his place. Logically they say it is philosophy that you cannot believe anything as it really is. You may say David can be someone else and vice versa. We make new patterns and distract reality by displacing people and displacing their characteristics as art."

We Express our Objectives through the Picture

It is the third day today and students start to explain their stories in brief, one by one, before they start making their films. Clara, a philosophy student, is first to go.

Clara: "Basically I want to picture the uniformity in work."

Kiarostami: "I suggest we only talk about what we are going to shoot. Theories come from work. We don't want to tell our goals. Rather we explain what we are going to do shot by shot. So this way we will explain the film we are going to make which was reviewed in our head, so start with the shot."

Clara: "I'll explain and tell you what I'll make. At the beginning I thought their jobs were boring and regular, but it was different afterwards when I talked to them."

Kiarostami: "I like to ask you all not to talk about your methods, rather say my film will start like this, and leave the other things to us, the viewers, so we discover whatever is in it. We should express our goals through pictures. I mean, we cannot give out brochures with our films. So to whom and how are you going to say your things?"

Clara: "My film starts with an image of machines and lemons."

Kiarostami: "Which machines? Which lemons? Where, in the factory? We had a factory which packaged lemons from start to finish. Which part of it would you start from?"

Clara: "It's still not clear to me where to start."

Kiarostami: "Then clarify it in your mind and tell us later."

"Filmmaking totally depends on getting over this part. Where do we want to start from? It is more like a speech, is it possible if I say that I have some theories but I don't know where to start. Our difference with others is to know where to start, what to say, and what not to say and how to end it."

Trust only What you See

He suggests using simple, reachable things. I personally agree and accept this suggestion because I have seen many of my friends make their work harder for no reason and they keep looking for things that are hard to find. This mistake is clearly seen in the explanation of the next student.

Student: "The film starts with hands planting some seeds, and then we find out he is planting lemons. Then slowly we see them grow and give fruit. We see the phases of evolution."

Kiarostami: "I don't understand. What do you mean by the phases of evolution?"

Student: "We see the trees growing bit by bit."

Kiarostami: "Are you making an animation?"

Student: "No, I will have pictures of the tree at different times growing."

Kiarostami: "So you take pictures of many trees and introduce only one, meaning they are that first tree?"

Student: "Yes."

Kiarostami: "Your job is a lot simpler if you define your scenario well. If someone told his scenario and you noticed he cannot convey his thoughts, it is your duty not to be satisfied, because the second he leaves this place he is accountable and responsible for his story, words are meaningless afterwards... I mean if he is going to make the film it is better if he has a cameraman and tell him to put the camera there and use that lens. So I think our fantasies about making movies should be limited to what we are going to express with what's on the screen, what it will connect to and what will be the next picture. OK, continue."

Student: "We see the tree growing and slowly bear lemons and keep seeing the hands at work behind all of this, so this will be a help to the nature."

Kiarostami: "I got it up to the part of the tree growing and since you don't have four seasons available now and must finish the film in one week, then I don't know about the tree blooming and bearing lemons, how do you want to do that?"

Student: "Maybe that factory has pictures of the tree blooming but I'm not sure."

Kiarostami: "If you are not sure then you are not ready to start. We are responsible for a film that is going to be ready by next week. We cannot talk about the things that might come true."

Student: "Most of my work will be showing the human hands."

Kiarostami: "But where? The hands have nothing to do when there are no flowers. Right now you see lots of hands around you. You tell us where to put our hands and we will. We have the lemons and our hands now. When we go see a location it means we see and understand all our possibilities, nothing more and nothing else, we have to work with available conditions, and not saying I need spring now for flowers to bloom."

Student: "You are right, I haven't seen that place yet, I would be more certain if I did."

Kiarostami: "If you didn't then you don't have the possibilities. That is why we go see the location. We are responsible to go and take a picture, not define a scenario. This is not a writing class. Maybe you should think more about what you have seen there, because you are not ready yet."

Student: "They are going to show me another place too."

Kiarostami cuts him off and says "There is no going to be, if that is so, then we see if we see. I am sorry if I talk this way, we don't have much time and this is for your own good so you don't go on the set and don't know what to do. Those people in factory have no responsibility and if you ask they will tell you politely, 'Yes, there are flowers.' They won't say no, and they won't say when. So do we have to wait for nine months? You only have to trust what you see."

Use Sound to Improve your Work

When most students define their stories, they are often unaware of the dramatic effect of sound in expressing their ideas. Sometime using high or low sound or adding or deleting can greatly change the concept of a movie. You will see this effect in the next story. This next student is going to set his story set in a lamp factory in Murcia.

Student: "My first shot is when the workers come to work at eight in the morning."

Kiarostami: "Have you seen the factory?"

Student: "I have worked there. We see the workers entering the factory and punching in their time cards. We have a black picture where we hear mechanical sounds then see the assembly line and the workers being busy. On the next shot we see one worker assembling the bulbs. I zoom in on his face and see his thoughts. I cannot tell all of it now."

Kiarostami: "Tell us."

Student: "For example, he says to himself, 'I forgot to take the garbage out last night. I always do.'"

Kiarostami: "I got it, later on we see similar scenes with the others? Then what happens?"

Student: "On the next shot we see another worker assembling. We see his face deep in his thought."

Kiarostami: "I understand, so we can conclude that we go into different workers minds and see them being somewhere else. Their hands are here working but their thoughts are elsewhere. Go on."

Student: "We go to a paint shop. I take a full shot of a worker painting. I take another of his face."

Kiarostami: "Is it the same thought shot or different?"

Student: "It's the same."

Kiarostami: "So the same thing goes on in the paint shop. Then we go to the packaging department and the workers there are also thinking about other things while packing the goods?"

Student: "Yes, but I still haven't been able to connect these thoughts together."

Kiarostami: "Is it necessary?"

Student: "I want to try."

Kiarostami: "OK, good. Try."

Student: "On the last part we take a shot of the factory ceiling with the sound of machines, the voices continue and these voices swallow up the machine's voices."

Kiarostami: "Great, good idea, so at the end the thoughts will take over the sound of machines. Very good. Then they slowly leave the factory, it is nice. Go make it."

Kiarostami whispers a poem from Hafez to himself, "I among many, my heart elsewhere."

He then continues, "Filming in the light factory, using a light bulb is good since symbolically ideas turn on with a bulb. Thank the workers in the factory and also on behalf of ministry of labor." (They laugh.)

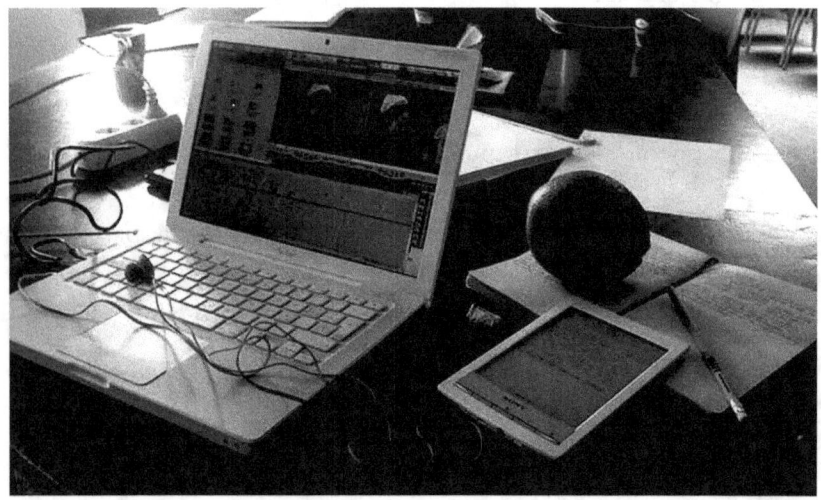
Editing in the classroom.

Our Duty in Cinema is to Delete Unnecessary Elements

These classes teach us that all elements that do not improve our story must be deleted. We shouldn't waste time on things that make no difference. For example if a tractor is going to pass by a few workers on the field and we don't have access to a tractor and that scene doesn't help the story in any way then we simply delete it. In the next story a Brazilian student, Janaina, explains her story and Kiarostami emphasizes the above point.

Janaina: "The title of the film is "Among Orange Trees." It begins with three people picking oranges."

Kiarostami: "See, now I want to know who those people are. Are they farm workers?"

Janaina: "Three farm workers."

Kiarostami: "Three men? Define and tell us what you have seen, for example three women working or three men, because it helps us to make the image in our mind."

Janaina: "Yes. OK, three men are picking oranges and there is a machine beside them working continuously."

Kiarostami: "What kind of machine?"

Janaina: "I think the one that cleans the street or a tractor clearing the path between trees."

Kiarostami: "So a tractor is passing by, on the corner of our picture?"

Janaina: "Yes. Then the tractor's sound gets louder and suddenly it dies. The driver gets out and starts to check the problem. The driver is the person who runs the farm. He talks on his cell phone at the same time and we show the three men still picking oranges. He finishes his call and tells the men he is going to bring someone to look at the machine. They feel easier when he leaves and come down from the tree."

Kiarostami: "What do you mean they come down?"

Janaina: "I mean they leave their job."

Kiarostami: "I have a question, if it is the season for picking oranges, then what is that truck doing there?"

Janaina: "He is taking away bits and pieces of wood and trash between the trees."

Kiarostami: "But it is not a good time for that now, I doubt it, it was you who put that truck there and logically when people are picking fruit no huge truck must bother their work."

Janaina: "Well maybe we can say I need a car to be there, something to put the oranges in after they are done."

Kiarostami: "Well you should have said that earlier. You say maybe we do, maybe we don't. We have no time for maybes, there shouldn't be any maybes involved. We have to go take it."

Janaina: "Well I do need a car there."

Kiarostami: "Why do you need a car in your film?"

Janaina: "Its purpose is that it breaks down and the owner leaves and workers stop working."

Kiarostami: "Well, do you have to bring in a car so workers can stop working? Can't his wife call him and say, 'Our kid is still at the school and you must go pick him up,' and then he leaves? I mean something easier, because this machine will cost us. Our duty in this kind of filmmaking is to delete all excessive elements. We have to put away all costly things which don't work and are useless for our film."

Janaina: "It is logical for me that when there is orange picking for a car to be there too, I think there has to be a car."

Kiarostami: "OK, but when you start taking the film you will notice how hard you will have to work finding a truck and how much you are going to pay to put it there, I am skeptical about it, so continue with your story, but you can find a much easier and cheaper way to have the workers leave their job. Go on with it."

Janaina: "All three sit down. One looks at the sky and another starts pealing an orange. One asks his partner if he has any children. He answers, 'I have four,' and takes out their pictures and shows him. He too asks the same question and the other replies, 'I have a girl and my wife is dead.' The third person starts singing children's songs to himself. The one who has the children splits his orange and gives half to the one whose wife had died and the film finishes."

Kiarostami: "Can't they do this few minutes of chatting during lunch, after lunch or during holiday?"

Janaina: "They are all in a situation under stress, hard work and don't have enough time for this… This is the only time they can find a little peace to talk."

Kiarostami: "OK, but I don't like your workers. (Every one laughs.) Because a laborer who has to do work must do work, but as soon as the owner leaves they stop working. Maybe you want to make it political, for example a protest against capitalism."

Janaina: "My idea was that when the machine stops working due to malfunction the workers cannot continue to work either."

Kiarostami: "Well what sort of philosophy is that? There were no machines for thousands of years and still laborers did their jobs. You are not expressing your subject clearly."

Janaina: "When there is no boss and no machine they feel they don't have to work."

Kiarostami: "Oh my, this belongs to a 50 year old Maoist book. What are you talking about? We want to make a simple and small film without any manifest. We are trying to picture a simple environment, but you have put so much burden on these three workers which make them completely unlovable. So much heaviness and little obligation if you want to defend labor rights, this method is a wrong method because it defaces the work, the image of work. Do you remember yesterday when we went to the sea and the boats returned and how hard the workers did their job? A laborer who does his job is more beautiful. We are talking on the basis of static in comparison to workers who pass the buck and want to see pictures of children. That laborer doesn't even have time to do that. That belongs to our breed now a days. I bet if you corner 100 workers in middle of a desert you cannot find a single scrap of a picture in their pockets. These are just our delusions. Think about your script a bit. I am not here to reject any script because you can make whatever you want, I just give you my opinion."

Janaina: "Do we have to do this work with the cooperation of others or do it alone?"

Kiarostami: "The idea belongs to one, it's yours. I mean someone has to take responsibility for it and others can help make it better but eventually the one who signs off on the idea is the director."

The First and Most Important Viewer of Your Film is Yourself

We always have this question in our minds as filmmakers "Should it be our goal to attract the viewer? And which viewers are we after?"

From Kiarostami's point of view the basis of cinema is to attract viewers, but the important thing is who those viewers are because there are different types of viewers. Kiarostami came to the conclusion many years ago that he could never attract television series viewers, so he never went after that because to him the idea was useless. None the less we have to consider an original viewer for ourselves and to see who they are.

"The first and most important viewer of your film is yourself. See if you can make yourself satisfied. If you can definitely satisfy yourself then there are definitely some viewers around the world whom you can satisfy, even if you don't see them. Maybe they are not among your neighbors or your friends but they are somewhere in this world if you are satisfied with your film yourself. But again it depends on many things, for example how much are you going to spend on your work or how much and how many viewers do you need? One of our tasks in these classes is to lower our cost so the number of viewers leaving the theater doesn't bother us. It is important to know where we stand. The trouble with all independent filmmakers is that they don't have

an exact definition of independent. They say, 'I am an independent filmmaker,' but they get upset when their film isn't shown in 30 theaters, and they get jealous of the ones that do. So if I am an independent filmmaker I should accept the fact that I might hardly have even one theater with limited seats. This is when we can tell ourselves and the viewers what to do."

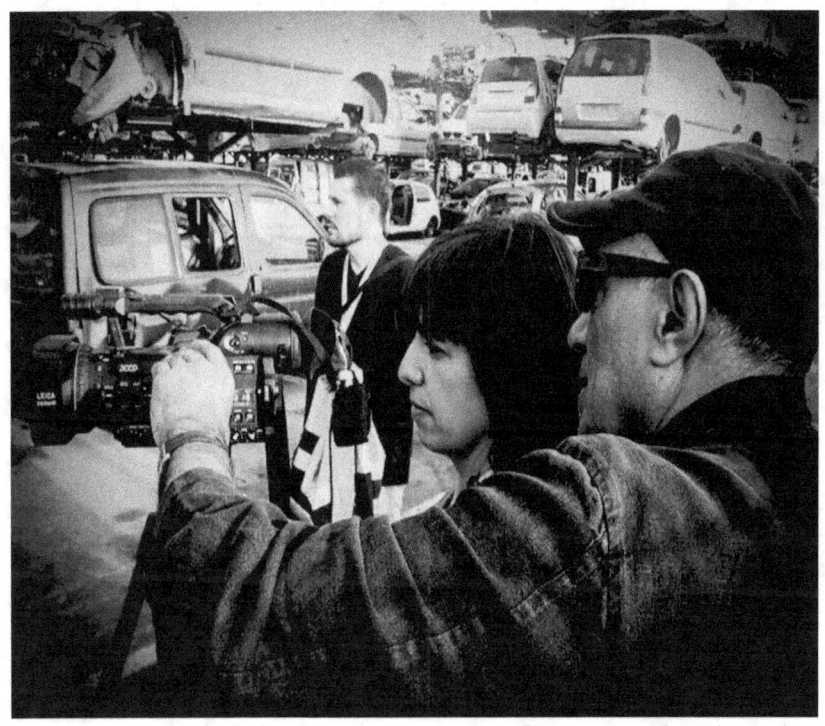

Kiarostami works with a student.

Try to Talk Edited

You can recognize a filmmaker whose thoughts are consistent and knows exactly what he wants to do right from the beginning. They avoid the excess because they must have a picture for each extra word or sentence. In fact they are getting ready for the most important part of their directing which is to edit, decoupage, the film.

Another student starts to talk about his film: "I want to make my film in four short sections."

Kiarostami: "Four short films?"

Student: "I start with a shot entering the beer factory and then I go to the section where machines are working. Two workers are talking while working. One says let's get together this afternoon. But the other one says this afternoon is not good, I have a date with a girl who is going to be my girlfriend."

Kiarostami: "In a beer factory?"

Student: "It seems that man is too optimistic about his date. On the next shot we go to the lemon packaging factory and there are two ladies having a similar conversation and one says I have a date with a man. There is a bar where the two are supposed to meet. They were introduced through Internet."

Kiarostami: "Where? Outside these two places? The same man and woman?"

Student: "Yes, outside. The same two who said they are having dates."

Kiarostami: "Tell me about that picture, what is it? How do they enter the bar? What reaction do they have when they see each other? How long do those shots last?"

Student: "10 seconds."

Kiarostami: "It will be better if you tell me how. I want to see your 10 seconds."

Student: "I have an open shot of outside. The guy enters first then the girl."

Kiarostami: "So they enter one after the other?"

Student: "Yes sir."

Kiarostami: "So this one enters the bar and then the other one? Please, tell me once more, tell it like decoupage, draw it on the board so I see how they enter. Do we see them up front or from the back or the side? Do they stay in the frame or go out of it?"

The student starts drawing the picture.

Kiarostami: "So the bar disappears when he enters and we won't see him?"

Student: "Right, we won't see him."

Kiarostami: "Do we see them introducing themselves to each other?"

Student: "No."

Kiarostami: "OK, good."

Student: "We go to the beer factory on the next shot but this time only the machines are working and we hear their voices talking about how his date was. He is talking to his friend."

Kiarostami: "What is he saying?

Student: "He says he didn't like the girl so much."

Kiarostami: "OK, good."

Student: "I go back to lemon factory like before. Machines are working and outside the frame we hear the lady saying that the man was dull and she didn't like him that much. Each one of them tell different stories, they both reject each other and tell their own point of view."

Kiarostami: "What do you mean they tell their own point of view? They say they didn't like each other, it's obviously their point of view."

Student: "It ends there."

Kiarostami: "Thank you. Go take it. You don't have to sit here anymore. Go right now and get ready for work."

"You cannot imagine how much it helps when you avoid extra words when defining your story and how much it helps your

film. If you cannot explain your story correctly then I doubt you can make it right, because you decoupage it by defining it. We transfer what's on our mind to the listener, find our mistakes, find our weaknesses and get to know the unknown parts. In my opinion if you explain your story correctly then you know exactly where to put your camera, your film will be compressed and you work with more control. The part of defining is the most important part of production, even more important than the script itself. An extra sentence becomes an extra shot and that can damage the film. So the sentence becomes the picture. Try to talk edited. Don't tell the unnecessary things but tell what we need to know from the start, like are they a man or a woman."

The World is Work and God is the Worker

Nayra, a Spanish student, tells her story next. "I will give you the picture but my story is about the last day of a lemon on a tree."

Kiarostami: "Thank you for telling your unnecessary sentence so short…"

Nayra: "My story has three parts and the open starts with a picture of a lemon field."

Kiarostami: "So your story begins form here, to remind everyone again that we can skip a lot of things that don't need to be said. From now on we will cut and put them aside. We will hear the story from the part of an open view of the field."

Nayra: "We slowly get close to a lemon who has the lead role."

Kiarostami: "You mean the garden has only one lemon or more?"

Nayra: "No, there are other lemons. We show that it is almost the end of the day. So for the shot we get closer to the lead role. At this part we hear the sound of nature and also the voices of workers. The next shot is taken from the top of the tree and the sound of nature increases and the voices disappear. Then a worker comes and picks up the last box on the ground and after everyone leaves we are left with the lemon alone."

Kiarostami: "You mean we are left with only one lemon? How long is that lemon in our frame?"

Nayra: "It is in our frame from the time workers leave. Then we change the shot and get a closer picture of the lemon and the night begins."

Kiarostami: "When you say a closer picture, do you mean we see the workers leave in the background and then the sunset?"

Nayra: "We don't see them. We know that by hearing the voices getting further away."

Kiarostami: "OK, we see one lemon. Can you tell me approximately how long this shot will be?"

Nayra: "Almost eight minutes. But other thing happen there."

Kiarostami: "Is the lemon shot eight minutes?"

Nayra: "No, no, I put the camera somewhere so the lemon is not in the frame. The camera is in place of the lemon."

Kiarostami: "So the camera is looking from the lemon's point of view."

Nayra: "Exactly."

Kiarostami: "Good, go on."

Nayra: "Night comes. We see the stars because nature has more presence. All the elements I talk about are controlled. Morning comes and still looking through the eyes of the lemon, there is morning dew and freshness. Then we see peels of other lemons and hear a faraway sound. A small dog comes in the picture, he is searching and then takes a bite from a lemon."

Kiarostami: "The lemons fell from the tree?"

Nayra: "Yes, then the dog's owner comes and he might be the owner of the field. He caresses the dog. The dog has a human name. He tells the dog to look around, here and there and then takes a lemon himself and goes. The lemon he takes is not the lemon of our story. Our lemon is still there. Then we will have a picture of things like ants and flies. Then we have a sound which reminds us of workers returning. Then it is time for couple of workers to rest. They go sit under a shadow to have their sandwich and they listen to the sound of nature."

Kiarostami: "I suggest a tea bottle in this spread too because it goes with the morning."

Nayra: "One of them lies down and we see the profile. We get all of this from their motions, the other one's cell phone rings. He talks then disconnects. The other one shows him a song on his cell phone. Then the whistle is heard, meaning go back to work. They both get up, talk a little and one takes the other one's hat off like they are joking. He doesn't like that and they go to a tree. He picks up his clipper. He snips two lemons, one of them is our lemon. Then on the last part we hear human voices. Then there is picture of the whole and the sound of workers together filling the boxes and the film ends."

Kiarostami: "I think it has a good environment. I have one or two problems though, I again don't like your workers like the previous story. We have a saying that goes 'clouds, wind, moon and sun are working so you may…' You showed us the dawn and the beauty of such a morning, but your people came and dropped and slept and no work. In my opinion we are dependent on nature and we must also compromise the nature of workers, the nature of the worker is to work."

Nayra: "Well I don't know much about the worker's world in the films. I wanted to know how they spend their regular lives."

Kiarostami: "No, when you are here, then they cannot be as themselves. They are at your mercy, I think you can go do your thing. See, I don't want to know about reality, when the morning comes sun comes up… ah, it has a bad feeling for me when workers sit and rest because I have been given a nicer picture of the working class in my life than what I have heard here in the past couple of stories. There is a poem that says, 'The world is work and God is the worker.' The way you described it you'll have hard time in this and I'll be happy if I see you take even half of what you just told us. If I were you I would think about it a little more, especially when you still have no location, do you know where your workers are working?"

Nayra: "Yes, I found the place."

Kiarostami: "Do you have the dog too?"

Nayra: "Yes I do, he is very gentle."

Kiarostami: "How about the ants?"

Nayra: "I don't have that one." (They laugh.)

Kiarostami: "Go break a leg, go take it."

Film Always Starts without an Opening

The next student starts and asks: "The introduction or the picture?"

Kiarostami: "Please start with the picture. You don't know how much you serve yourself and the cinema by not giving any introduction. When you don't give an opening then you are compelled to give a better picture of your idea through images and that is more pleasing, but when you give an introduction then you tell yourself well I told my idea and they understood, and when it comes to making your film you don't know how because the film always starts without an opening. Films start suddenly. It doesn't have any introduction. OK, please go on with your plan."

Student: "The picture starts with the white thigh of a cow and a black hand going over it."

Kiarostami: "Good for you, so far so good, thanks a lot. Because now we have the picture."

Student: "The hand moves on the cowhide as if to give a feeling of affection. Then the picture opens slowly and we see the worker. He is leading the cows to their places to milk them. Then we move down to the worker's feet and his dark green boots. We hear a sound of a tractor while he is moving the cows and then we see part of the truck backing up. The tractor has a trailer and is entering the place. Milking starts. One empty bucket of milk is a bit dirty and he starts cleaning it. Then we hear the sound of the tractor going away. When it is gone we see it's tracks on the ground which are white. Then we see the road with the same white tracks. The worker keeps putting the milk in the storage. Then we enter the slaughterhouse and see a big cow being chopped. We see the entrance of the slaughterhouse with the white tracks of the truck. Then we see the man feeding the cows. Then he changes his clothes. He takes off his dark green boots and puts on black shoes. Then we see the same man going into a butcher shop to buy meat and when he leaves the store we see him leaving white tracks on the ground."

Kiarostami: "From his boots or his shoes?"

Student: "His shoes."

Kiarostami: "The first part of black hands on white cowhide was good and I want to see more of that. So without any rejection I say maybe instead of going and chopping up the cow in this story, the man puts a milk bottle into his child's mouth and the baby is looking at the camera then it ends. Black hands holding a white milk bottle is nice. Your films must have a theme in it so it doesn't become a documentary, any small idea will do. I don't mean fictionalization, but have an ending in such a way that the viewer feels more satisfaction. I think you can start your work."

Have Self-Confidence

Kiarostami believes when we think we are doing everything the best way, that is the worst time of our lives. We must understand that our power comes from our weaknesses. We must find our weaknesses and not be overcome by them. We must also enrich our forte to reach self-confidence, this is not related to filmmaking alone but it is true in everyday life. We will see in the next story how Kiarostami admires the self-confidence of a student.

Student: "I want to work in a shoe warehouse. My picture starts with the closed doors of a warehouse and the camera is waiting for someone to come and open the door. We wait, a car comes, the owner gets out and opens the small door of the warehouse. Then a truck comes and a worker gets out. Then another worker comes and the last one checks the big door. After this section, the camera is going through shoe shelves. Someone gets in front of the camera, he is a worker picking up a shoe box. The camera was taking blurry shots until the worker picks up the box blocking it."

Kiarostami: "I don't understand."

Student: "It wasn't a part of the scenario but I decided to take it any way." (Everyone starts laughing.)

Kiarostami: "We are glad you're not taking it too. Go on."

Student: "At the same time the workers are talking and saying that recently the cops have become careful and they fine any small incident. The camera at this time shows another section where a worker is filling up a big box with small shoe boxes to send away. He is looking for a pair of shoes which a store asked for, but he doesn't find them and argues with other workers. Finally he comes near the camera in which a small part of its picture is covered by a shoe box and he picks it up and by doing so he puts both the camera and the other worker at peace."

Kiarostami: "And the viewers too." (Everyone Laughs.)

Student: "Right."

Kiarostami: "Does it end there?"

Student: "That's the frame work."

Kiarostami: "You tell the story with such confidence that I think you must make it as you tell it. So I won't say anything. Go make it because I really want to see it."

Student: "I have made a part of it already and want to finish it."

Kiarostami: "Great. Go, finish it. I haven't made any judgment on your work because I am so affected by your confidence. So I want to see the film. Please go and don't stay here."

The student leaves with complete confidence.

I was curious to see Kiarostami's reaction when the student finished the film and showed it to him. Kiarostami really liked it. He used to say some things surpass our mentality and we have no record to compare them with, but they are good and so there are times when we have to give them credit and importance because there is no basis for accepting or rejecting what you don't know you have. This is exactly what most critics do not consider and they completely reject what they don't understand. Critics sometimes have a very short reaction to anything original. Kiarostami gave credit to these sort of students and gave them the opportunity to make their films because he believed no one can tell for certain which work is bad.

The next student rises to tell his story and Kiarostami cautions him to avoid extras.

Student: "The workers of a lemon factory enter the factory through the same door that we see the machines."

Kiarostami: "So you shoot their entrance early in the morning, right?"

Student: "Right, that is it."

Kiarostami: "So far so good, it has a good mood to see them coming and changing clothes. Good start. I hope they don't sit and take a rest between putting on two sleeves." (Everyone laughs.)

Student: "They go to their places and machines start up."

Kiarostami: "So far it is very good because we haven't seen this part. Because we haven't seen them before the work and that moment is a mere eyeful than seeing them at work."

Student: "Then we see a boy and a girl at the start section where lemons come, they put them on the machine and the lemons continue going to different sections and at the end there is a boy gathering them and packing them for exit. The boy and the girl we saw at the beginning do not talk to each other at all, but the last boy and the first girl keep looking at each other."

Kiarostami: "Very good."

Student: "In the part when they are separating the lemons, there is a machine working which resembles a human heart." The student takes his camera up to Kiarostami to show him his take.

Kiarostami: "It is good."

Student: "He comes close to show it fully."

Kiarostami approves and says: "It is like a human heart. Are you going to put that in middle of the two characters?"

Student: "Yes, this machine is like the heart that makes the relationship between the two, it beats for them."

Kiarostami: "Very good, go make it."

Student: "It is not done yet, there is more."

Kiarostami: "And you are going to add the sound of the heart for sure."

Student: "There are lots of sounds there and they cannot talk to each other."

Kiarostami: "You can slowly turn down the sound of factory and raise the sound of the heart."

Student: "That is a great idea."

Every one laughs because it seemed the student had taken Kiarostami's place. Kiarostami turns to the students very seriously and says, "Well I need affirmation too. That is good."

Student: "I'm not finished yet."

Kiarostami: "It is good up to here, don't tell the rest and let's see it in your movie."

The students is happy and sits.

Kiarostami: "His idea is good and also his performance. One can trust you by your voice. You just might know your work. If you want to go you can."

Student: "I would like to stay and listen, I'll go later."

Kiarostami: "No problem, please stay."

Clara, the philosophy student, stands and is ready to tell her story once more.

Clara: "I am trying to straighten out what I said before."

Kiarostami: "Thanks."

Clara: "I want to explain shot by shot. Shot1: I start from outside the factory. It is dark and slowly the sun comes up."

Kiarostami: "Which factory?"

Clara remembers that she has not mentioned which factory she meant.

Clara: "Lemon."

She continues by explaining each shot, calling them out one by one in their order.

"Shot 2: There is a machine which the workers put the lemons on it at the start."

"Shot 3: We see the belts and chains moving but the lemons are not on the belt yet."

"Shot 4: We see movement of the machine going up and down."

"Shot 5: Then the movement from side to side, still no lemons on them."

"Shot 6: With a close shot we see lemons entering the machine."

"Shot 7: We only see the worker's hands putting the lemons on the belt."

"Shot 8: From above we see the lemons moving on the belt."

"Shot 9: We see the worker's faces with smiles."

Kiarostami: "How did they look smiling on that day?"

Clara: "When I asked them if their work was uneventful they said 'No, this is our work and we are happy doing it.'"

Kiarostami: "I am worried that they might be compelled to smile. They should be in their natural mood, go on."

Clara: "We see the lemons going and moving in lines. We see them dropping. The first workers were women and these hands belong to men. Then we see the boxes from above moving. These are all shots to make a rhythm that we can montage together later on. Then we take the shots from the side instead of above and at the end we see them packaged. We see the workers helping in the packaging.

We see from the front that lemons come and go in the packages and at the end the sound gets cut off. We go out and see it is dark."

Kiarostami: "Considering that someone else has done the same loving path, the difference between your film and the other one is your taste and selection of camera angle, which one is nicer do you think? It seems we have two similar films with one subject and I yet don't know which one will be better."

Clara: "I don't want to work on the factory alone. I want to do this film with my shots and editing and the high and low sounds."

Kiarostami: "Well it is very good, but it needs a small point and in order not to become a documentary, your's ends at night, you should do something for the end and find a good ending. The way you explained, it means you know different angles, but you must go early morning because taking these shots will take a lot of time."

"Considering these two films, I should say to others who want to work in this parameter to choose another subject because it has become limited, unless you add more stories to it. In the other film there was a romantic message from one person to another, now you should find something else to add because this factory doesn't have the capacity for more than two films. Of course we have another one starting with workers entering the factory and so that makes three films so far. Any way it doesn't matter if we have three films because we are learning through example. Each one is working on his own movie but don't forget that there are other subjects too. For example about the trees we saw on the way here. There are gardens full of fruit. There are gardens like the ones picked, now see how much we can play with these? There was also a garden with dried out branches with no leaves. For example a garden that has it's fruit picked bare suddenly and the leaves fall. Maybe someone loses someone else and since we haven't seen the time of picking then there can be stories at that time so we don't have to go to the factory. In this case the workers have to be interesting because it is original. Take a look and consider these tomorrow."

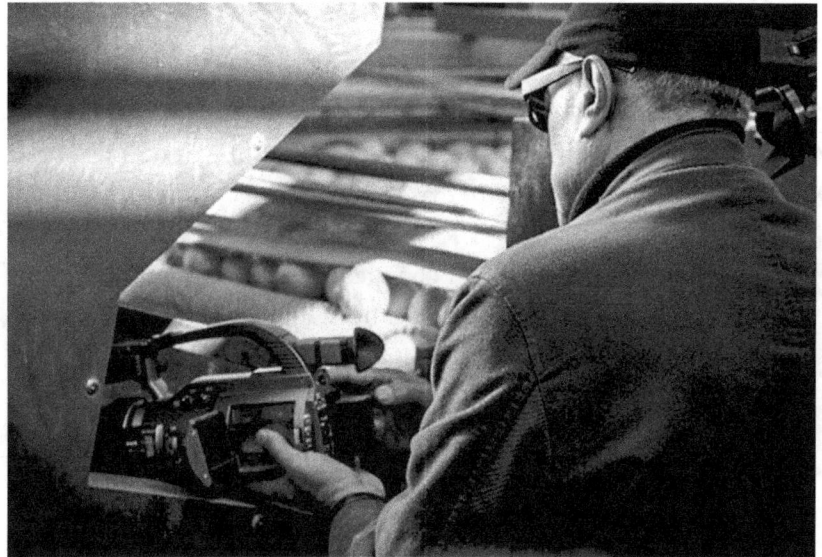

Kiarostami in the lemon factory.

Directing an Actor's Performance

The next student is the same one who wanted to think about his story more and is ready to explain it now.

He stands and starts: "I changed my idea and now I want to make something about the cattle ranch. It is early in the morning and a big, strong, black man arrives at the ranch and goes to another man, who is white, and much smaller than him to ask him what he can do."

Kiarostami: "Where is the white man?"

Student: "In the same ranch."

Kiarostami: "Is he a stranger?"

Student: "Yes. He asks, 'What are you doing here? What can I do for you?' The man looks at his face and looks around then says, 'I am new here.'"

Kiarostami: "A new worker?"

Student: "Yes. But new."

Kiarostami: "You said new, does this new mean a worker? You should have said a new worker. Our work is done faster if we use our words carefully."

Student: "The second one wants to know who he is since he is new around there. In the next shot we see the new guy has put on work clothes and is following the other guy to see what he is supposed to do and he shows that he likes to learn, but it is obvious he hasn't done this before. He is careful where to put his feet and where not to. The other man is showing him different jobs, things to do but the problem is that the white man's cell phone keeps ringing. One time his phone rings and he wants to answer it but the guy turns and gives him a look so he tells him that he will be quick. Then another time a call comes and he says on it that it's his first day and cannot talk, then his mother calls and tells her he has a new co-worker, the next one is his wife and he tells her everything is going well and it is a good job, he asks how the kids are doing. At the same time he tries to make conversation with the guy and keeps asking if he has kids or not, but he just does his job and answers shortly every once in a while. At the end of the day they change clothes. The white man shakes the other's hand to thank him for his help. He shakes his hand and tells him it was a good day and asks what they are going to do tomorrow, his cell phone rings again. He laughs and turns it off. The first guy says they will see each other tomorrow and leaves."

Kiarostami: "I think it's good. I think you can play the role of the white man who keeps talking on his cell phone very well, right?"

Student: "Yes, I am fascinated to be both actor and director at the same time." (Everyone starts laughing out loud.)

Kiarostami: "Your job is easier because you know what you want and you can direct the other man."

Student: "You are right."

Kiarostami: "Directing in front of an actor means you are teaching him as an actor too. I just think the film's rhythm should be a bit faster. I mean the calls need to be a little bit more. When you started to tell your story it reminded me of another one and I want to explain it to you and if you want you can make it."

"A black man is running as if he is doing a 100 meter race. He is running real fast to milk the cows because as you know when their milking is delayed they yell because they are in pain. So it is completely logical that he is running just to relieve them. That is because we have always seen black runners. The thing that we don't know why he is running will be a bit satirical for the viewers at the end since this time is not for winning but to milk the cows. One minute of a film can put good effect on people, sometimes a minute can effect more than any 10 minutes."

Kiarostami tells the student that he can go and start his work and tells him again that he is good for the role he wants to play.

Nothing Helps you Work more than Deletion and Selection

Now the students are trying to avoid the extras and talk edited. Instead of explaining their objectives they begin by only defining the pictures and let us discover the message though the images. Most of them know that adding extra shots would make their work better, but selecting the best part is the only way to help their story.

It is time for another student to explain his work.

Student: "My story is also about a cell phone. It starts with a face of a woman around 30. She is talking on her cell phone and she seems angry. There are flowers around her. At the same time we hear another person coming into the picture and he asks if she has the Margarita flower. She puts the phone away and the shot opens. We see it's a flower shop. She tells him, 'Yes, we have the Margarita flower,' and shows him. The customer wants them and she starts preparing them. He then asks, 'Do you have sunflowers too?' She doesn't respond because her mind is elsewhere. He asks again, 'Do you have sunflowers?' She says 'Excuse me, no.' He pays and leaves. She picks up the phone again."

"The next shot is on a lemon field. A cell phone is ringing. Some workers are coming and going. We don't know whose cell phone is ringing until we get close to a man's hand picking fruit. The ringing gets stronger and we see it belongs to the man but he doesn't answer it. We don't see his face, but we see his neck sweating. The phone stops ringing."

"A man comes up to him and says he has 10 minutes to rest. He picks up his bag, goes to the lounge and takes out a lemon from the bag. The phone rings again. He has no reaction. He punches and tries to squeeze the lemon into a glass. The phone rings again. He adds a little sugar and some water, picks up the glass and at the same time decides to answer the cell phone, there is some silence, then we see the face of the flower saleswoman. In the next shot there is a woman on the phone saying, 'Excuse me.' We go back to the picture of the worker but only seeing part of his body holding the glass. There is more silence and he leaves the glass."

Kiarostami: "Are his 10 minutes over?"

Student: "Yes, I think so, yes."

Kiarostami: "So why did we have to see the woman in the flower shop? You could start with the worker and finish with him. A woman saying excuse me to someone, that's it? What difference does it make who that lady is?"

Student: "I want there to be an angry lady."

Kiarostami: "All of that is in her voice. A lady who is calling all morning and no one has answered. Well, a man trying to ask for pardon from that woman, it is obvious she will be angry. Her voice shows it too. So what do you want to show beside regular chats with this sales person? Do you have sunflower or not? What is this dialog good for? Your work doesn't have movement. Later on you will see how hard your shots will be, but you know best. If you want you can make it but nothing helps your work more than deletion and selection. What not to take, when to say what, does it help if you delete this part or it will get worse. It is best if you don't see the lady on the cell phone. Her voice is enough because if you show her then I want to know more about her. Why is she excusing herself? Because is she more important than the flower saleswoman? Her selling flowers doesn't help us at all. It is a bit old fashioned too, but do as you like."

Student: "No, I really liked what you said."

Kiarostami: "But you know what you can do? Put your energy on the man who sweats, not by watering his T-shirt, but by really having him work. I mean he takes the burden on behalf of all the workers resting, making them embarrassed." (Every one laughs.)

"Yesterday when Mahmoud was filming the workers in the fishing port, their faces had great beauty while pulling the rope and fastening the boat to dock. Their bodies had nice complexity in their figure, like Rodin's paintings. That's what you must take. I mean each frame of 24 in a second can be a nice picture of the sweat on his skin. Resting is closer to death. Now I have nothing to do with your work if you like your workers to rest, but from an aesthetic point of view, working is nicer than resting. Resting is like death and that is why I say we can add the meaning of work to it. Again I remind you of the poem that says, 'The world is work and God is the worker.' I think if you go to real gardens you see this, even the lemon packaging and factories, to see if a fruit is rotten or not, this is not really work and a little girl can do it too. The picture shouldn't be the way to say well we are busy working but our work isn't worth a penny."

Student: "Well it helps me a lot that it is a *she* in my story and it will be more logical and at the same time more mysterious."

Kiarostami: "When you find your location, I think it's best if you put your camera on a tripod and don't mention which worker has the lead role, see who works best, who is more interesting, then chase him with the lens, going, coming, putting boxes here and there, taking them, then you can add the phone call to it. I mean make a documentary then turn it into a story, and at the end tell him to put the cell phone in his pocket and go. Lead him at the end, don't lead him during the scene. I mean choose a worker whom you like. I am telling this from a woman's point of view. A look of a woman to a worker, and if you found an admirable one, then follow that person and if he wants to rest then tell them to film themselves." (Everyone laughs.)

The Ending of your Film must Give Something More than the Rest

We usually have a strong part in our mind that either is the end or the beginning because we choose a subject according to the image in our mind and it starts with that mentality, but the important thing is what we want to say with that image and how we want to finish it. Kiarostami puts particular emphasis on this.

It is time for Juliana, a girl from Mexico, to describe her story.

Juliana: "In the port there are some men. We see them from behind and cannot say exactly what they are doing. We see a boat slowly moving closer to the shore and seagulls are circling above it. They are busy doing their jobs."

Kiarostami: "See now, I think we all saw your film yesterday. Now tell us what you have added to it."

Juliana: "For a moment the boat moves out of the camera and we see the workers out of frame but the seagulls go and start pecking on the water."

Kiarostami: "Good. It is important how to finish because if you go there and only take something and did not think about the last part then you cannot finish the film. The last part of the film must give something more than the rest."

Juliana: "I saw the fishermen dropping something in the sea for the seagulls and I wanted to film that moment."

Kiarostami: "That's great, go break a leg."

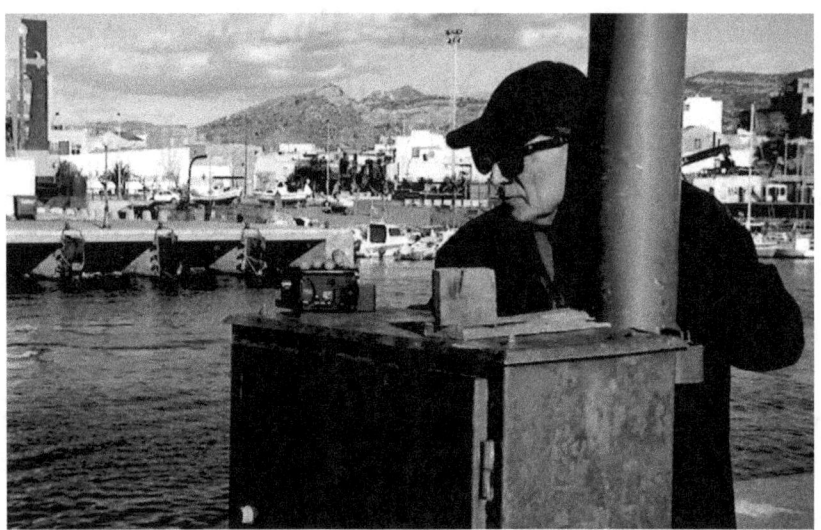

Abbas Kiarostami at Cartagena fishing port near Murcia, Spain.

We must Shorten Everything for Better Communication

Kiarostami believes that in our era when one's feelings can be transferred by a single SMS then we must shorten all our explanations because now is the time for short themes and if they use the same feeling in their story then the film will be more successful.

The next person comes forward to tell his story. He is from Brazil.

Student: "My story is very simple."

Kiarostami: "See, this sentence itself is extra, we have no choice, we must learn."

Student: "I want to talk about the touching sense."

Kiarostami: "This is extra too."

Student: "And I want to talk about the atmosphere of a place."

Kiarostami: "You are still talking extra. I am waiting for your story to begin."

Student: "But I want you to get ready before I explain my picture."

Kiarostami: "Let me tell you why these sentences are disruptive. Don't think the problem gets resolved if you put them aside. These will cause you to make mistakes. You cannot communicate with me through them, we want to consider your film as simple and secretive and it will not help if your explanation doesn't come true later on in the film. You are using these sentences to help you get away with something and it shouldn't be that way. If you know they don't help then forget and delete them, just give us your picture plainly. Because these are like catalogues, people either like your movie or they don't, they do not read the catalogue."

Student: "I get what you mean, but there is a girl in the factory separating the lemons. The girl is the actor. I want to say how this girl enjoys her work in this environment and touching the lemons with her hands."

Kiarostami: "We too want you to say this, but through pictures."

Student: "Certainly, the girl arrives at the factory…"

Kiarostami: "But she was there already."

Student: "I'm telling it from the start. A girl, our lead, enters the factory. She goes to the changing room and changes. She picks up a nail file. We also use a sound effect so we know she is filing her nails."

Kiarostami: "Where? In the factory?"

Student: "In the changing room. She is waiting a little."

Kiarostami: "I am worried the owner of the factory doesn't see this." (They laugh.)

Student: "She then starts to walk in the factory, and goes to her place and separates the lemons on the belt as they have told her. As she works, her co-worker keeps talking, but she wants to concentrate on her work. The co-worker keeps on talking and she shakes her head as confirmation. We put some lemons there with different colors."

Kiarostami: "I don't understand what you mean by different color lemons."

Student: "Our lemons have different colors, and these don't."

Kiarostami: "So you paint the lemons?"

Student: "Yes, we color them. When the colored lemons arrive she wants to pick them quickly and she is also careful nobody else sees her taking the colored lemons. So naturally other lemons are passing and she continues. This goes on and her co-worker is still talking. Our shot changes to outside and we see her going through the factory leaving and looking at the boxes. Inside one of them there is a rabbit instead of lemons, I mean it's hanging… (He means inside the factory as the boxes move up to get filled, students are now starting to laugh). She tries to take the rabbit, somehow, so no one else sees. She changes her clothes, leaves the factory and goes toward a nearby farm. She is holding a bag and takes out an orange, she peels it very slowly, feeling it classically then it ends."

Kiarostami: "Good, make it. Let's see what comes of it."

Be Aware of the Story

Kiarostami again emphasizes on telling the story through images not words. We have a much higher responsibility when we explain the story through pictures. We get the story either by pictures or literature and we cannot delete the story as simply as we want to.

Student: "We are in middle of a road at night. It is dark everywhere and we see an open gas station. We hear sounds from inside, radio, refrigerators, these are all taken with a Tele lens. We get closer and take a picture of the surroundings. For example the reflection of light on the gas spilled on the ground or a few lamps here and there, dry places or foot prints or the garbage people left. We still hear the sounds saying it is three in the morning. A young man arrives and sees him working with his computer and he is the only one person there."

Kiarostami: "Is he inside or out?"

Student: "He is in the gas station office. When he finishes his work, he goes and cleans the floor. He then changes the radio channel and reads newspaper. He walks around and time goes by."

Kiarostami: "How long has is this so far?"

Student: "Two to three minutes."

Kiarostami: "That's good."

Student: "Then we hear sound of a car getting closer. The sound increases. He puts down the newspaper and turns down the volume of radio. He is in himself all the time. When the car arrives he moves in front of the glass and goes to collect the money. We are seeing all of this from the Tele lens."

Kiarostami: "Very good."

Student: "I put the microphone inside the place. The car comes into frame, stops in front of a gas pump. No one gets out and he comes out to see what they want. The window lowers and we see this in the picture. When he comes out we hear the sound of outside, like he is carrying the microphone with him. We hear the sound of crickets and so on. He pumps the gas quickly and takes the money. He is now alone outside. He is looking at the car driving away and the sound lowers. He goes inside, changes the TV channel and we again see him from distance and again the sounds of radio, TV and refrigerator. It ends there."

Kiarostami: "You must be very interested in this tone if it satisfies you this much. What is obvious from what you explained that you have thought about the details, but there is one more thing, the film doesn't move along. I mean nothing happens between the start and the ending. If you hear the story from the audience's point of view they would say there was a man in the gas station he came out and pumped gas for a customer and went inside again. If this is interesting then you have done a good practice for your film, meaning this is a part of a longer movie which you did very well and it is not easy doing this part with such interest. This is pure cinema and I think unfortunately and especially in times like these that our cinema is dependent on a story. But any way let's see a shot because you have been so careful about details that I think it will be a good film. Your story is more consistent with my personal taste than my responsibility here, because I always suggest my students to be careful with their stories because you cannot cut the story so easily. I made my first movies just like you and now I have come to the conclusion that story is essential."

Student: "I tried to tell the feelings of a person, he sits there until something happens, but nothing happens except a car coming and going."

Kiarostami: "I know, but it is not enough for a short film. This is good to be a part of a long movie, because in a longer film we get the idea that nothing is happening but in a short film it gives a notion of an unfinished shot. Again it will be a great practice. It will be great if you make it as you explained. Thank you."

Student: "Should I find something for the ending?"

Kiarostami: "It will be great if you do. You can have another person come and when he gets close, he can put a bullet in his chest then he drops on the ground. That's an ending too (he laughs)… It is dark (he laughs)… and then he cleans out the cash register and leaves. No. I am joking, that is wrong. Do as you said."

Kiarostami was influenced by his personal world and wanted him to do the work and see the result. He believed this film was only a section of a whole and it makes us to wait for something to happen, the atmosphere itself was anticipating, waiting for, an event to occur, especially by the information given to the audience.

You Shouldn't hurt the Viewer's Beliefs

The next story belongs to another girl from Mexico. She stands and begins talking about her idea. "We are inside a boat moving real fast and the sun is slowly rising. Five fishermen are preparing their net and they drop the net in the water as they go on, and maybe spatter some food for the fish to come. Then we see all the fish jumping up and down and also seagulls circling the boat. They start to bring in the net. We zoom in on each body while at work to see their strength pulling in the net. Then we see the fish jumping up and down. We see the hands of a fisherman who is beating the fish with a stick to die. They are bleeding and the blood mixes with the surrounding water. I move the camera over the fish. Some of them are dead and some alive. The camera moves to the hands of a boy who is picking the live ones, puts them in a bucket and empties it into the sea."

Kiarostami: "There is a boy there?"

Student: "Yes. The boy wants to do it again and the fishermen are doing their job. He is happy with what he is doing until someone yells and calls his name, José, he turns his head to look. The man tells him not to do that and to go on with his job. He puts down the fish and goes on the deck to take water. Our ending part is the shot of fishes jumping up and down."

Kiarostami: "Who is the child? What is he doing in the boat?"

Student: "He is one of the worker's kids."

Kiarostami: "Is it logical to take a child to the sea?"

Student: "Yes, I saw it yesterday."

Kiarostami: "How old was the child?"

Student: "12."

Kiarostami: "But a 12 year old doesn't do such things. If he is a fisherman's child he knows the rules of fishing; that they must take the fish to market to sell. Your boy is a city boy not a fisherman's. The story is good but hard to believe. I saw the child you are talking about too. He is a working boy and a working boy knows the rules."

"The atmosphere is very good but you just have to make it believable. Your child doesn't belong to the sea, he is from the city. But try and see what you can do with it, maybe a younger child and we should know it is his first time in the sea for some reason, maybe he was alone at home or… it should be obvious that the environment is new and interesting to him."

Student: "My problem is I cannot have any dialog and want the sounds of nature because I have no microphone."

Kiarostami: "Don't take the boy we saw. Take a six or seven year old child to justify that it is his first time for not working, he is not a worker. It is not important there is no dialog because you should know what is going on among them. Find a father for him so he can work with him."

I remember in the past that Kiarostami used to say that it is OK to import something to the story which doesn't have particular logic in it, like the fisherman who catches a baby from the sea. Now for some people a question comes to mind and that is "Why do we have to follow logic regarding this child?"

Kiarostami says it doesn't make any difference to him since both come from the same contract we make with the audience in the beginning. A contract not written and not heard that our film has such an atmosphere and we must give it in the first few shots. For example in here our sea is real, our fishermen are real and also time is real, so importing something unreal disrupts the logic. If we do want to import such things it should be done early in the film because we cannot see the film as a documentary at first then suddenly see something outside of our beliefs. It would be OK if it is believable but we resist against it unwillingly as soon as it blemishes our belief. So in the story when a fisherman catches a baby from the sea we are making a story out of reality from the beginning. Another example is in the works of Márquez when he says the man was killed his blood passed down from the kitchen to the ditch, crossed the street and went up to that house. This is a lie and we know it is not true. It is an illusion out of reality and that is why, for example, surrealists have found a firm stand in art because they say realism has no place. As Godard said 'Life is a badly made movie.' So surrealists say they change life by taking reality to a world where fantasy also interferes and they combine fantasy with different aspects of reality.

The Picture Separates Itself from Literature

A Girl from Barcelona begins her story: "We are in the lemon field."

Kiarostami: "A field?"

Student: "We first see that place and then the workers working. From the whole process of picking the fruit, boxing them and putting them on truck."

Kiarostami: "Have you seen this process? We didn't, have you?"

Student: "No I didn't."

Kiarostami: "You didn't… but I think it was such, go on."

Student: "Even if it isn't, I think this is regular thing they do."

Kiarostami: "I say it is too. I just wanted to know if you have seen it or not."

Student: "At the end of this chain we get to a worker who keeps saying thank you. He thanks anyone and everyone who does something and others get upset about it. They are a bit tired of him saying thank you. One of his co-workers says, 'I wish you were like my cat, quiet and silent.' He goes to get another box and when he returns he sees a cat in place of the man. He keeps calling out the worker's name."

Kiarostami: "That's cute. Was this a real joke or you made it up?"

Student: "It was a joke between workers. They kept giving things to each other and the guy kept saying thank you, thank you."

Kiarostami: "How did the image of the cat come into your mind?"

Student: "I saw many cats when we went to the field."

Kiarostami: "It is not important if there is a cat or not, you can take one with you there but the ending is like a fairytale, not an ending of a movie. It is like old stories not like a film."

"How could he wish for him to be a cat and be silent when this is not going to happen? He could just say, 'Shut up. We are tired of you.' It is not the ending that it should be, even if it is, the cat is good for the story not for the film. Think of something else for the ending."

Kiarostami stresses that a film starts with an image and ends with one. The image must tell the story not literature. Cinema that depends on literature is only good for television series, where watching is useless and just hearing it is enough, but it is not like that in cinema. You cannot even blink because you must pay close attention. So our story must suit the cinema. Of course you can make films from these stories but it also won't hurt if you don't. These stories have the same efficiency as their definition, like stories of Mulla Nasreddin, in fact like all the stories that have a happy ending and have a message or advice. It is not necessary to make a movie out of these because the picture separates itself from literature and your narration will not add anything to the story. Now maybe you use accessories or clothing to give it antiquity like many television series but that will not add anything to the story and also no audience will have the opportunity to get to a personal conclusion from your story.

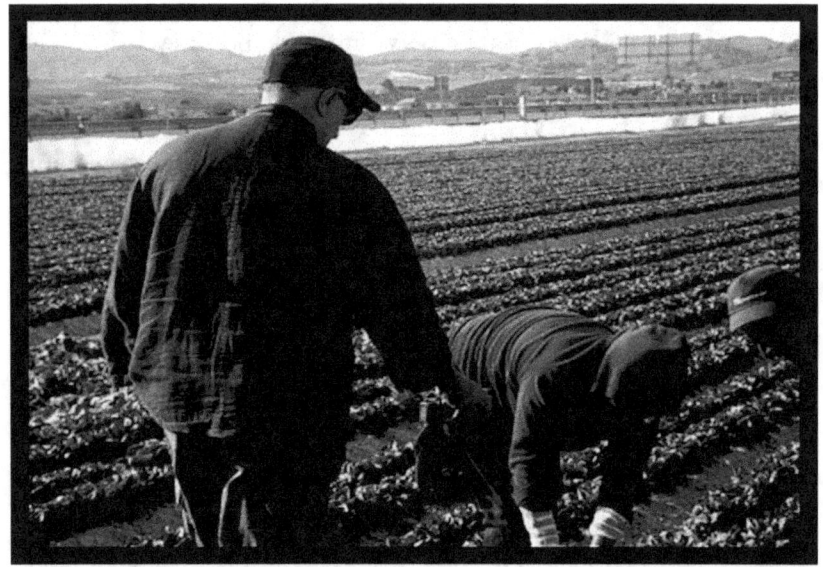

In the fields surrounding Murcia.

Stories are Everywhere if You Look Hard Enough

One day we arrived at a dump yard when we went to look at locations with Kiarostami. He liked the place and wanted to go back there with the students, maybe to find stories there, but no one had any ideas when we arrived. We just kept looking around at this huge place with all the wrecked cars. They still had no ideas when we returned to the class. Kiarostami had an idea, though, and said he wanted to make a film about the dump yard.

The group was excited to hear that from Kiarostami and to see how he will make it. He chose a boy and a girl from among the students. Kiarostami had Mark, the male student, put on a blue suit and gave him a toolbox. Then he asked me to follow him with my camera in middle of the dump yard through the cars and into the alley. He also asked other students to film the scene from different angles.

Mark walks through the cars searching. He stops picks up his cell phone and says, "Tell me exactly where you are." Then we see him from another angle finding the location among the wrecked cars, he gets close to one of them and opens the door. There is a beautiful girl sitting inside the car and she asks Mark to please fix the mirror for her. The car is a wreck and doesn't have anything, not even seats or wheels, but Mark fixes the mirror with coolness, the girl thanks him and she looks in the mirror to fix herself up. She then turns on the car, it starts and she drives away, like all its problems were fixed just by fixing the mirror. After a lot of searching Kiarostami found a clean car just like the wrecked one with the same color. He put it in the place of the wrecked one when it was time to film it moving. It took one day to film and it was a big lesson for the students by teaching them that one can make a good film without a big budget or facilities and by deleting extra elements. The important thing is to look carefully. He called the film "Mirror."

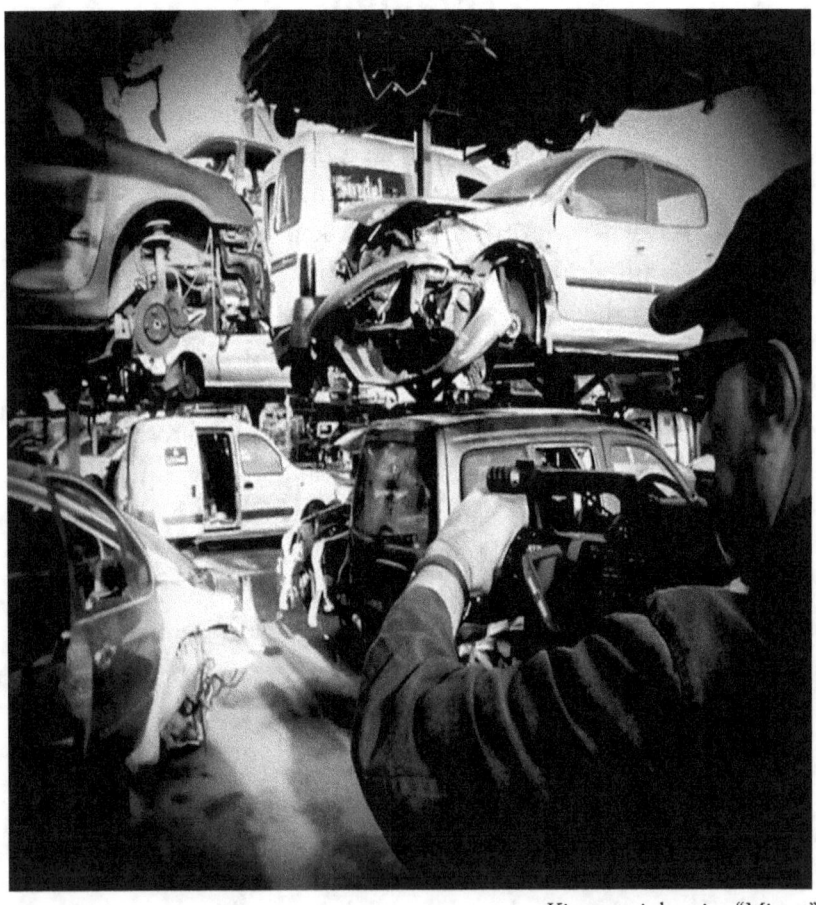

Kiarostami shooting "Mirror."

My Father Killed Himself with Work

A student from Murcia got up next and began explaining his story. "Antonio is a farmer. He has his father's bag which was left to him after he killed himself. Antonio's crop hasn't been good this year but Antonio has a picture of him from his childhood taken around the time of his father's suicide. He always carries this picture with him and it is like a charm which he really believes in."

Kiarostami: "OK, then?"

Student: "That's it, should I explain more?"

Kiarostami: "Well, how should I say this? This is an idea. How do you want to tell it through pictures? What will we see on the curtain?"

Student: "It starts with showing a closed bag and then we see him working in the place where his father took his life."

Kiarostami: "We didn't see his father committing suicide and now we only see a bag. We have no idea about his father and you must tell us that through picture."

Student: "Well we will find out later."

Kiarostami: "How will we know? Should we just wait until later?"

Student: "The man works in the warehouse."

Kiarostami: "OK, this Antonio works in a warehouse and takes out a wallet, right?"

Student: "Yes, right."

Kiarostami: "What does he do then?"

Student: "I haven't done the dramatic parts yet, I am going to do it later. I just want to explain my story."

Kiarostami: "You should have done that, but if you know then good enough, go and make the film because it is a low budget movie but also it is your responsibility to have what you just defined in your film. If I were you I take the shot of the worker who is busy working and suddenly looks at the camera wiping his sweat, takes out his wallet and shows it to another worker and says, 'This is a picture of me when I was nine, the day my father took his life right here in this warehouse.' You have to say he committed suicide with work otherwise we cannot relate it to the story. You may also do it any other way you think. What I just said was another version of your story. Maybe he puts back the wallet and goes back to work without rest, or something else as you see fit. This is just one version of it. I felt good with the story because my father died from excessive work too. He also killed himself with work. He was 62 when too much work killed him. So the story is not fake but real."

Kiarostami talks to the students about other locations such as the beer factory for example. Afterwards he asks, "What about it? Who has thought about this?"

A couple of students raise their hands. They have thought about the place.

Kiarostami: "I have an idea about that beer factory if anyone is interested. We can have that place complete with no workers. We film the whole process of the bottles being filled and capped by robots and we don't see any humans working. At the end there is big, strong robot picking up huge packs of beers at once and putting them aside. Then we see a hand taking a half full bottle of beer, bringing it up to his mouth and drinks. The hand belongs to a worker standing outside the factory. You ask how he is and he says, 'Good, but forced out of work, the robots have taken over and all the workers are out of job.' The place we went to only had three engineers and robots were the workers, a jobless worker drinking beer made by a robot, while resting, because there is no work and they are resting. (The students laugh.) Anyone interested is free to make this film."

A girl answers: "I will make it if no one else wants it."

Kiarostami: "Then you may start, but remember it needs a clean take from the whole process up to the end of the chain and especially when the huge robot comes, to make that comedy, a bitter comedy."

You must Turn your Knowledge to Personal Knowledge

One reason students feel real easy and learn quickly in Kiarostami's classes is that he doesn't put pressure on them. He doesn't like to negate educational methods used in most schools because he believes these might be the only means of learning for young students. The experience of doing more than 20 workshops has proven to him that teachers in this field put too much unnecessary pressure on students and that most graduates are unable to make any movies due to so much needless information and if they do make any it will be a potpourri borrowed from elsewhere. Before making their first film, he wishes that students could bang their head somewhere and forget what they have learned and gain some creativity instead. He always cautions them that their knowledge must be ingrained and be set so deeply in their mind that it helps them unknowingly during filmmaking, not by remembering. He always suggested that knowledge must turn into personal knowledge which is different for each person and is private.

"I'm not against knowledge and having information is great but most cinema graduates 'know' but 'cannot.' You do not have the right to use that knowledge until it is yours and it becomes personal. That is why their works are mostly collective."

The next student is from Cordoba, Spain and begins to explain his story: "Louis works at dairy farm where he milks cows and feeds them. We start in the farm, shooting images of the place where the cows are lead to be milked. The milk pumps get attached to their breasts one by one. We see a corridor where a few naked girls are, their breasts are noticeable and they take the place of the milking cows. This is not meant to be erotic or sexy but I want them that way."

Kiarostami: "I understand exactly."

Student: "Louis is standing there when they are bringing in the cows, he separates one from others in the story and then it ends."

Kiarostami: "Very beautiful, you know what you want to say in your work. Go and take it, I see your work better with a fish-eye lens. The open lens shows the whole figure. If I were you I would use one lens for the whole film. When the cows go to feed use an angle lens, it makes it more beautiful, and the lens makes a bit of deformation."

Student: "Take the whole story like this?"

Kiarostami: "Naturally the deformation is less when they are at a distance and more when getting closer. So take with one lens, but it won't always become the same. This is just my idea. You can do as you wish."

Video Art: Turning Fantasy into Reality

Student: "We start with fixed shots showing some stores and merchants."

Kiarostami: "What do you mean? I didn't understand."

Student: "It starts with fixed shots, four seconds each of a pharmacy, a milk factory, a store…"

Kiarostami: "OK. Each shot is separate."

Student: "In the background we hear the sound of cars coming and going. In the next shot we see someone who just woke up and is recording something on his cell phone. He says, 'My name is… and I am an astronaut. I come in at eight and leave at 10.' This shot ends and we go to another person recording himself saying, 'I'm a veterinarian.' The same thing goes on for the other people. In the next shot the man is at his job explaining his work saying that he controls satellites. The others also have similar jobs. In the last scene all four are seated around a table talking. It is Friday and the work week is over. They are talking about the past week and each one is talking about their real jobs, the one that said he was an astronaut actually works at a public pool. My idea is about when we are kids we want to be this or that, but when we grow up we end up doing something else."

Kiarostami: "That's good, but we have to make judgment with the actual film and if I say how good or bad it is right now it's just to show what possibilities the film has. When we see something we don't understand we tell you to go and work on it, so when you hold the camera in your hand you will know what you will shoot. Now, it is not important if it comes out good or bad. So in order not to be limited with my subject of *worker* I reminded of a poem again that says, 'The spider had started its web before sunrise.' Even if we have a shot of a spider making a web in beautiful sunlight then this is good for part of our work. Even the ants that work so hard can be a part of our film, work is not limited to humans only."

Student: "I will talk to the four men so they record themselves and give it to me."

Kiarostami: "Whatever you like, that depends on you. The second phase is your own ability. Again there is another poem which is nice 'The workers union finally did not recognize the spiders work.' This is a poem by me."

Another student starts to tell their story.

Student: "I should say that when my film is ready I want to show it on two monitors or curtains."

Kiarostami: "You have mentioned that before. There are films that do not have a story line and they are called video art. So there is no need to repeat video art. You may start because logically it is hard to make video art understandable. So do your work and any way we expect to see video art from you, not a film story."

When I was in Tehran, I went to Kiarostami's studio in the basement of his home. He was working on a piece of video art with two of his students. He was deeply involved in creating a thought that even he wasn't sure of its ending. The picture was of the shore far out to horizon and a few seagulls laying eggs on the beach with the waves lapping at their feet. He had taken one shot of the sea alone and the film of the seagulls at another time and place standing there laying eggs. He was mixing the two videos together and he didn't know how long the picture would be. He said he is now into video art more than before, it is like a dream to him.

"When someone sees a dream and wants to define it, we cannot have a proper reaction against his excitement because he has seen it and not us. The same goes for video art as we cannot define it with any words so we have to transfer the feeling. When someone tries to explain a dream, all his worry is how to transfer what he has seen with words, and that is why people who make video art say I have an idea but it has to become a picture because that world is quite personal and cannot be transferred through words. So they convert it to a work that we can see."

Kiarostami wasn't sure the students who wanted to work on video art could express their feelings through words for our perception. So he let them have the opportunity to make their film first and then see how it had come out. For the video art he was working on that day I visited him, he used to say the work is reality to him but it is not reachable so easily and that in fact he is converting a dream into reality. He had not seen those seagulls by the shore at all but he said it cannot be so strange when a little displacement is applied and the possibility exists.

I am Still Looking for a Walking Stick

One of the students is a young Spanish guy who had made a film about Rumi and also had attended the Cannes film festival. His name is Oliver and he asks Kiarostami: "You said you wanted to share beauty with others, so why do we put a camera between our life and ourselves? There is a story about Rumi which says, 'When a blind man sees he doesn't need walking stick.'"

Kiarostami repeats the saying, thinks a little and tells Oliver to ask his question once again but more plainly and clearly.

Oliver: "Why do we put a camera between ourselves and beauty?"

Kiarostami: "Why shouldn't we?"

Oliver: "Because the camera limits beauty."

Kiarostami: "Then how do we explain what we have seen? No camera is used in literature but words are used. Any way everyone has some way of expressing themselves. You used Rumi's saying 'When a blind man sees he doesn't need walking stick.' You transferred this to us through words. Rumi used words as medium. I use the camera as medium between what you and I have seen. But what do you suggest?"

Oliver: "Beauty is certainty and it's greatness should expand."

Kiarostami: "How? We have pictures and words as mediums. What do you suggest? Do you believe in transferring something from someone who has seen to someone who hasn't?"

Oliver: "I don't intend to question art."

Kiarostami: "I am not asking you to question art. I am asking what is your suggestion?"

Oliver: "I sometimes think like Rumi, to throw away the walking stick and be with what we see."

Kiarostami: "So what are you doing in this class?"

Oliver: "There is a haiku that says 'You ask yourself, you answer yourself, poor soul, I am still blind.'"

Kiarostami: "OK I accept, but the difference between you and me is that I am still looking for the walking stick. I haven't gotten and will never get to the status of Rumi but I think all of us here are looking for that walking stick. Rumi was after events. I am not after events. Any way there have always been exceptional people in history. Sometimes they cannot be our idol because they are so exceptional in its true meaning. I, as a small person, keep looking for that walking stick to go easily on this path."

Sometimes the Story is too Much

There was an old castle on a hill close to the fishing port where we went to visit a location one day and one student was left with its image still on his mind. He now wanted to tell his story.

Student: "We have an opening, like a picture of the fishing port we went to with the castle on top of the hill with a fence around it."

Kiarostami: "Is the picture of the castle with the fence around it your starting shot?"

Student: "Yes, there is someone going up there very fast. The path is kind of rough but he gets there any way and we see he is young boy. It is his first day of job to look after the castle."

Kiarostami: "His job is to protect the castle?"

Student: "Yes."

Kiarostami: "Have you been there?"

Student: "No."

Kiarostami: "I saw that castle from below."

Student: "Me too."

Kiarostami: "Look, I doubt that castle needs a young boy to protect it. Go and see if this is true. What is he protecting it from?"

Student: "It doesn't matter, this or any other, there are lots of castles in Murcia that are being protected and you can only visit during certain hours because they have guards protecting it."

Kiarostami: "Then it can be this way, OK… We are now inside the castle, go on."

Student: "The guard from the past shift is worried because this new guy is late. He takes off his suit and gives it to him. His gives him the hat and keys too but they are heavy because they belong to the castle. He just tells him to be careful that no one enters because he is in hurry to leave."

Kiarostami: "How do you know it is his first day guarding the castle?"

Student: "From his dialog with the previous guard."

Kiarostami: "Good, right."

Student: "The castle is among the protected national monuments and there is sign on it that says: No Entrance, Even You. The boy is now alone in there. He starts to look around here, there, up and down to see what is going on. He looks across the fields and to the sea below. He is little nervous about his job because he doesn't know exactly what his job is, but he begins to like it as we move on. He walks through the castle like a prince looking down on the whole city far away."

"He takes an afternoon nap, (everyone laughs), when it gets colder and when he wakes up he hears something. Usually there are ghosts and spirits in castles so at first he hides in fear. At the same time he feels responsible because it is his first day, so he goes to see where the sound came from. He goes to a corner and sees a ghost."

Kiarostami: "What does he see?"

Student: "But these ghosts are not from the past, they come from Senegal."

Kiarostami: "What are the things we see? They certainly don't say they are from Senegal."

Student: "He only sees two shadows with blankets on their heads. It is not important that they are from Senegal. They are hiding in the corner of the castle."

Kiarostami: "So how do we know they are ghosts?"

Student: "We don't know that either. The boy thinks they are ghosts because he sees two dark objects with blankets over them. They all get scared when they see each other. The boy didn't expect to see any one there and they were hiding so no one could see them. One of the men gets up to explain their story and tells him they are from Senegal and says, 'We have no home and no place to stay.' The boy runs away as they are talking and we see him leave from where he came from, running down the hill."

Kiarostami: "So he gives up his job and leaves the place."

Student: "Yes, his first and last day."

Kiarostami: "Then if it is so, there is no need that he goes to them nor an explanation that they are from Senegal, but just to see the ghosts from distance and run away. So if they explain their story then he should stay and not run away. When those two get scared of the boy there is no need to run."

Student: "Well yesterday the workers in port told me they were from Senegal and that stayed in my mind to say they are from Senegal. When we see them there, it is like the western movie duels."

Kiarostami: "Yes, but when something doesn't work for your film you must put it away. We, too, remember lots of things about those workers in the port that of are no use to us. Now you have to go find a castle. It was good seeing it from below, now you need to find the rest somehow. It is a bit too long and complex and has too much extra. Sometimes the story is too much. Well you have thought about it so go do it."

Kiarostami didn't like this story at all and the student didn't start making his film for a few days. When we asked him why he said he was still thinking about Kiarostami's suggestions. When the film was ready we saw that he had deleted the extra scenes and changed the story. It was now about a crazy, mad man who went up to the castle and would throw rocks at the pedestrians below. In the end it became one of one the better workshop movies and even now, a year after the workshop, Kiarostami still remembers it.

Cinema doesn't Need so much Strange

The next student comes forward. Kiarostami says: "Would you like to guess are his workers working or resting? (Everyone laughs.) Let's see."

Student: "It is afternoon in orange field and a girl is picking oranges alone."

Kiarostami: "It is beautiful so far because you are easy with work. There are many girls here, you can ask them to come and play. Films that are made easily make me happy because cinema really doesn't need so many strange things. Go on."

Student: "The girl has slow, pompous moves and keeps looking around."

Kiarostami: "So far so good, but God help us for the ending." (The students laugh.)

Student: "We stop there. The next shot is in the day, in the same field and scene with the owner explaining to a boy about his first day on the job."

Kiarostami: "I don't get it. Start from the beginning in short."

Student: "The second shot is of the owner talking to a boy who is starting his first day of work."

Kiarostami: "Where is he, where is this happening?"

Student: "In the same scene he is explaining that these people are working here and this is where you work. He points and says that the woman over there is his wife who sometimes comes to pick oranges. This is the husband of the same woman who was picking oranges suggestively yesterday."

Kiarostami: "OK, I got it, and he tells the boy that he can go and take as many oranges as he can carry with two hands."

Student: "I got this when I saw them talking yesterday that it is common for them to take home as many oranges as they can with only their hands. We go back to another afternoon, to the lady picking oranges and the new boy picks up the lady with his hands. It ends there with the boy taking his boss's wife which is as much as he could take with two hands."

Kiarostami: "You mentioned this as a common custom, but how would you tell that to the viewer?"

Student: "The owner of the field explains it to him."

Kiarostami: "It is good, but does he have to say she is his wife? Is it necessary she be his wife?"

Student: "Yes it's necessary because the boss gave the permission to take a handful and he is taking a handful of the boss's wife."

Kiarostami: "The problem is that it is more like a joke. I'm not talking about morality but why should he tell the new worker that is his wife over there? Couldn't she be one of the working girls? I think it is not necessary like your first shot that only one person goes and picks oranges. It is much nicer if you have several girls picking oranges. It is like a joke but you must tell it correctly otherwise it will not come out good. It is not real and must be kept that way. For example the girl turns and slaps him but he tells her, 'Well, they told me I am free to pick as much as I can carry with my two hands.'"

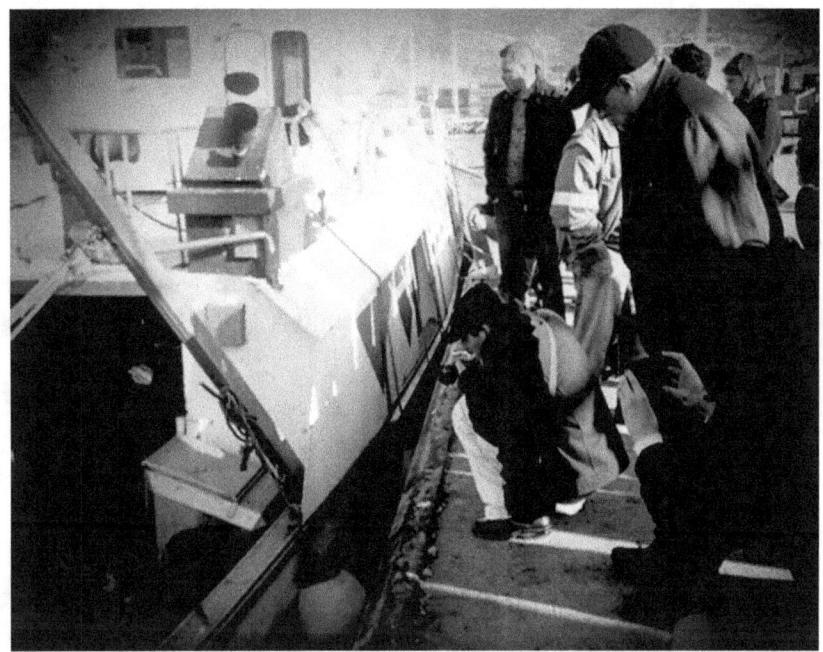

Filming at the Cartagena fishing port.

We shouldn't Impose Anything on Our Characters

Another student stands: "We are in an orange field and see two workers who are tired and they now enjoy some rest for a while."

Kiarostami: "How are they enjoying? You enjoy now, think that you are one of the workers."

Student: "They stopped working and are talking to each other."

Kiarostami: "Good."

Student: "Something disturbs their conversation."

Kiarostami: "What happens?"

Student: "This is what I haven't figured out yet." (Every one laughs.)

Kiarostami: "I will help you with this part and you tell the rest."

Student: "The problem is time stops but they are still there."

Kiarostami: "Doesn't the film have anything more to say?"

Student: "I haven't got anything yet."

Kiarostami: "Well think about it more and let us know."

Student: "I have to go there to know them better."

Kiarostami: "Well let me tell you right now, imagine a light bulb drops right in the middle, between them."

Student: "I don't know what to do. I haven't seen those people."

Kiarostami: "It is too incomplete because it is just the start and we only have two workers and they are not even working."

Student: "They did before."

Kiarostami: "We didn't see it!"

Student: "But it is felt in the film."

Kiarostami: "You have only shown the time when they are tired. They say one day a man painted something and it was white, like a blank piece of paper. They asked him, 'What is this?' He replied, 'Two snowmen.' They asked, 'Why can't we see them?' And he replied, 'Because the sun came and they melted.' Just like your story, because we don't see it, we only see two workers resting. Something must happen there. You have to make it."

Student: "Yes I have to make it, for me, I have to go there and see."

Kiarostami: "I can see two workers with the same idea of resting. They are sleeping in back of a bus and the bus leaves and keeps honking. When they wake up the driver asks them where they are headed? It has a good look, a few workers laying down on the seats showing they are tired. Of course if you intend to show the workers as being tired, otherwise you cannot. Now think about it and explain later on. I am still thinking about the one film that had the loving message through the lemons from start to end, with the heart, because it can be done nicely."

Student: "I have another story with the same orange field beside the factory. There are a few workers picking oranges. At the end of the day the boss tells one of them, an African man, not to show up tomorrow because he has enough workers. It is tomorrow and when the workers come to work, the one he told not to come shows up again."

Kiarostami: "Good so far."

Student: "The boss asks him what he is doing there. He replies, 'Yesterday you told me not to come to work because people are buying fewer oranges and you didn't need as many workers, but maybe today the world changes and people buy more oranges.' The boss looks at the worker with doubt. The worker goes, sits in middle of the yard and waits. Time goes by."

Kiarostami: "How does it go by?"

Student: "We know it because it was morning when he sat and now its afternoon and sunset."

Kiarostami: "Good."

Student: "The worker sees a car coming from afar and when it stops a gentleman wearing a black tie gets out and calls out to the boss. They are talking and the man is looking at them from distance. The boss looks at the worker still sitting in the middle of the field. He gets up, smiles and the film ends with him thinking the boss has a job for him to do."

Kiarostami: "Does he think the car came to provide some kind of work for him?"

Student: "Yes."

Kiarostami: "It is bit out of touch."

Student: "It may not be like that and he thinks there is a job waiting for him because he is a foreigner who doesn't speak Spanish."

Kiarostami: "We have to think something too, take something because how do we know there will be a job for him? We have to do the thinking. He can think, but not without us. We have to think there is a job for him and we cannot. Your scenario is good up to the part when the boss asks why he has come back. Maybe he can reply that he heard on the news the economy is getting better and that he thought maybe the boss heard it too and wanted to keep him. The boss can say with a smile, 'Well, go ahead work for today then we will see about tomorrow.' A little fantasy wouldn't hurt anyone. We need to limit our fantasy and it is more believable if the boss says comedic like to do your job for now, we will see about tomorrow. You need to solve this somehow so we can believe."

Student: "And we can end it right there."

Kiarostami: "Oh yes, add something better when you find it, but if not then end it like that. Your problem is that you do not have the right idea but you keep looking for a logical solution. You resist something that is not there."

If We want to Hear We must Learn to Be Silent

Your work is hard at first when you are with Kiarostami and it gets tougher if you don't put your trust in his ability to teach and train because you learn much more than what's related to cinema when you are by his side and in his classes. At least it has been like that for me and during the time I spent with him I came to the realization that one must fix oneself first in order to know what you want to do. You have to concentrate and avoid all extra things around you that do not help. On the first day when we went to see a location he had a strong encounter with one of the students who was talking on his cell phone and he told everyone to turn off their phones. He made an agreement with all students not to discuss or talk about anything other than the subject of work. You only need to accommodate him by opening your mind and senses for the next 10 days and he will open the doors of new world to you. He always says it is impossible to find what you are looking for if you don't clear your mind of useless things. You must concentrate your eyes and ears to see and hear what you want.

"In Iran sometimes I go out of town by car with my students. I have my camera with me and we always agree we won't talk about anything other than our subject. We keep our silence and sometimes it gets real bitter, but that's our agreement and it's good. So by keeping our mind focused on the subject we keep discovering new things. When we close the valves, the pressure

builds up for what is required and the stories start to fabricate. If we want to hear we must learn to be silent."

Another girl comes forward to tell her story.

Student: "We start with the beginning of the chain in the lemon factory. The workers are putting the lemons on the belt. We see the fruit has to go on a path and for a moment we get to the part where the bad fruit are separated automatically. Then we follow the good ones going to be packaged in boxes, small boxes which go into bigger ones. There are female workers who take out the bad lemons. One of the workers goes to pick up a bad lemon to put it in the bucket but it accidentally drops on the floor. When another worker comes to take away the bucket, the wheel on his cart kicks the lemon and it rolls across the ground. Other workers don't notice it and keep kicking the lemon. The lemon goes around and eventually stops at a lemon tree. Then we see hands entering our shot and they pick it up. There are some workers sitting there and right there they eat the fruit."

Kiarostami: "Again the workers are resting? You were good right up to this last part, but one lemon is not a watermelon to be fed to several workers. I don't believe that." (Everyone laughs.)

Student: "No, there is a tray of fruit."

Kiarostami: "But by this way they have no more connection with the story. Logically the way you had the story going I expected the ants will eat the fruit. People being there is not real to me. If you give it to the ants they will have a full meal otherwise it is not believable."

Student: "Why don't the workers eat it?"

Kiarostami: "See, it was worthless. You made this fruit worthless, people kicked it around. You said it was rotten too, so logically it shouldn't be noticed so much. You, yourself, pictured this fruit to get out of the cycle and an animal must have it. The workers I see here are definitely handed full bags of fruit at the end of the day."

Student: "So as you say I should change the woman, for example there is a bag to take away the fruit but when they come to take it away they think it was thrown out."

Kiarostami: "The path you saw up to the field had no problem but the ending must be fixed. You don't know what to do with this fruit, not where it came from. You already showed where it came from. If ants like lemons I would have you finish it with ants, but you have to sweeten it with sugar and they'll gather and eat it in three minutes. Find a way to finish this up in the air ending."

You Can give Story to a Documentary

Some of the students had documentaries in mind but didn't know what to do with them. Should they make up a story and impose, adding it to the location we were supposed to go or do something else? Kiarostami knew exactly what was going on and in fact he has professional methods for this which we can see clearly in most of his works. When we watch his films we sometimes wonder if it is a documentary or a work of fiction. Kiarostami believes that a documentary is not enough. It needs something else in order to be different and not a duplicate.

We arrived at a fishing dock, the other day, on the way back from seeing different locations. A few good looking men were repairing their net. One of them had attractive eyes and with his strong arms was sewing the net. I went closer to take some film of him and we chatted a little. Kiarostami also moved closer towards us. The young man was telling us that he has been there for ten years. He lived alone, had a Spanish girlfriend but there was no opportunity for marriage. However he wasn't worried and you could see satisfaction in his eyes.

These few minutes had its effect on us, Kiarostami was moved and said to me, "You and I have to go out to the sea with three of them tomorrow morning. It will be great to surf on the waves and throw you overboard. Maybe we will sing and they will sing for us too. I don't know what will be but do you think that is enough? Bringing in the net, that's interesting, catching fish is good."

Kiarostami, whose mental light bulb is always on, suddenly had an idea. He asked me, "What will happen if there is a five month old baby in middle of all the fish?"

My eyes sparkled and I began to think that the documentary could completely change and move towards a different type of cinema. I told him that this is a strange, beautiful idea but what logic could it hold?

Kiarostami said, "We are in the land of Márquez so let's think like Márquez. It doesn't need much logic and it will be full of beauty and mystery. Think about it, we catch a breathing baby from the sea amongst all the fish. The other one asks if he is wet. He puts his hand on the baby and says that 'Yes, he has wet himself.' He then says, 'I don't want it.' He asks the other fisherman, Abdollah, 'Hey Abdollah, do you want him?' He replies, 'No I already have two on my hands.' I think it is somehow natural to catch a baby from this sea. So the baby goes from one hand to another. Another asks, 'What is it?' They tell him that it's a baby and ask if he wants it? He replies by telling them to 'Put it there by my clothes.' Everything is so natural to him, very natural. They put the baby by his clothes. Abdollah is working and suddenly they hear crying and one of them says, 'Hey Abdollah, the baby is calling you.' So it belongs to him now."

The story that began as a documentary now ends with beauty and with a touch of logic. I don't need to say where the baby came from and how it is possible because this place is not real; it is more like a dream and is any dream real?

Kiarostami was right. It was then when I told myself this kind of filmmaking is for personal enjoyment and discovering myself mentally without following any specific logic is exactly the same kind of children's stories that Kiarostami and ourselves have always wished to reinvent. The same children's stories we made up and liked in our youth. It didn't matter if they were real or not.

"There are some Eastern & Iranian stories out there that I don't know how much you can believe them. We, Iranians, have a poet called Baba Taher Oryan. He was a wanderer who didn't have a home. One day he was passing by a school and saw some people reading the Quran with such beautiful voices. He opened the door and went inside, because he was a bit crazy too. He asked, 'What are you reading?' They reply, 'The Quran.' He asks, 'How did you learn it? It is beautiful.' One of them gets up, throws him out telling him that they broke the ice on the pool and then went inside to learn, then they close the door on him. It was winter and after a few minutes they hear the sound of a splash. They go out and see him in the pool full of ice. They take him out, dry him and warm him up. He is shaking and he says, 'Now bring me a Quran. I want to read it.' They give him one and he starts reading for real. Story is story, but it is not so much without reality and it could happen."

"One example is my film "Close Up" that man was daydreaming and who knew it could come true. When I saw Sabzian's picture in two cinemas I told myself, 'See, one little lie turned into reality.' He wanted so much to be important and he became so. There is nothing more realistic as that because we cannot resist any more when we witness a beautiful and funny dream. Any way you need to bring in a story to the world you see, and that is our part of creativity. Inevitably we have to make it interesting and add a story to it. You can find a story for any documentary, you just have to activate that playful part of your childhood spirit. You must become a kid again and then see what you can come up with."

Another student wants to tell his story and stands.

Student: "The first general shot is from the lemon factory. It is of a worker putting the boxes of fruit in a truck to take away. We have another general shot of women preparing the fruit to put into the boxes."

Kiarostami: "You mean we go from the end to the start?"

Student: "Yes, we see them do repetitive work and they are silent. At the same time we see the fruit falling on the table where they are working. Then we take a shot of the fruit coming toward the camera. Here the camera is taking an open shot and we see the perspective of the machines. We follow the path of the machines but against the lemon."

Kiarostami: "I don't understand when you say against the lemon. As a filmmaker you can put your camera where the fruit come toward it, get close, or you put it where they go away from you. What do you mean by against?"

Student: "They come toward the camera."

Kiarostami: "Better now."

Student: "We then see the same work, same sounds repeating. We get to the two people from the beginning separating the bad fruit, again repetitive work in silence. The other man stops working, the camera fixes on him. He picks a lemon and with a marker puts an X on it then puts the lemon back on the belt. Now the camera moves the other way, going forward with the lemons."

Kiarostami: "Let me understand and know what is going on because I don't know which way is which."

Student: "We see the same path but not in the direction of the lemons."

Kiarostami: "So this way you are showing the film upside down or backwards. You shoot this film on this path and then show it again, from the end to the start. I know how you will take it. Otherwise you have to take the direction of the belt from the other way around."

Student: "All of part one is the a shot of the lemons coming towards the camera. Then in the next part we have is a shot of them going away."

Kiarostami: "So you just change the place of your camera, change the angle, not the path. Lemons go in the same path."

Student: "We now follow the lemon with the X."

Kiarostami: "So we follow it with another angle."

Student: "Yes we now find the path of our lemon with the X."

Kiarostami: "Yes, good."

Student: "We go after it until it reaches the ladies we saw at the beginning because the film goes from the end to the start. The lady gathering the lemons is a bit off because she is talking at the same time to the one next to her, she picks up the X'd lemon without noticing it and puts it in the box. The worker picks up the same box puts it in the truck and returns. Then the picture goes back to the ones standing and separating the lemons. Then this man takes a lemon and stops working, our next shot is the same X'd lemon."

Kiarostami: "So finally, where is the lemon that went in the box?"

Student: "I saw that they were always working with the same lemon."

Kiarostami: "I don't mean that. The idea must come out of the same details. I understood so far that a lemon got marked and went among other lemons and nothing else happened to it."

Student: "It's path is a circle and it keeps going around."

Kiarostami: "Well I didn't get it but I hope your idea comes out well. The marked lemon goes in a cycle that you cannot reach to tell your idea. Can't you do something with this mark to make something happen? Maybe put a heart on it and it goes and goes toward that woman, she picks it up, smiles to the man from afar because your way is kind of confusing."

Student: "My idea is a passing work."

Kiarostami: "Your idea must come out in the picture which it doesn't, you are making your work complex."

Student: "I want to say this system has a message system."

Kiarostami: "But who got this message? First of all an X mark is not a message. It sounds like a desperate message and any way who got the message?"

Student: "First I had another idea for the X but I couldn't do it."

Kiarostami: "Do as you will, but it is useless. Go make it. I didn't understand anything from your explanation, but if you know what it really is then tell us through the picture so we get it too. If I want to define your idea I would say a man takes out a marker puts an X on a lemon and this lemon then disappears in middle of all others. Now who is going to get your message, we don't know. It is more acceptable if it goes to someone whom we don't know and that is good. If this is what you want to say then good, but if there is something else then I have to see the film and cannot comment on it like this."

Student: "I will try to show my idea in the film."

Kiarostami: "Maybe it is hard to explain it now but naturally you must make it and you may know what you want to do but it's lost in there somewhere."

Student: "I thought this worker thinks he will get fired for what he has done."

Kiarostami: "But why? The poor guy hasn't done anything. I think the best way is the love message marked on the lemon and it gets to the hands of that lady and she takes and puts it in her pocket and it ends. You are making your work much harder and cannot do it if you don't like the idea of the heart, let someone else do it and you will see how much the effect can be quick and spontaneous." The student looks away halfheartedly.

Kiarostami: "Go and make what you want and we will see it."

Oliver, the student who was making his film about Rumi, stands again: "I don't want to tell my story upfront because I still haven't found my location and I would like to do that first."

Kiarostami: "Then wait till it finds you."

The students laugh but Kiarostami is serious.

Kiarostami: "I hope the location finds Oliver because he was the only student who didn't make any movie and no one saw his work."

Epilogue

The next day the students began to make their movies. You could see and feel in them an inexpressible spirit. You could also sense a new spirit of competition within the group as they went out each day. Kiarostami and I would visit them at their locations over the next few days and I noticed how they would gain strength and confidence when they saw him. They only had a few days to film and every morning they would go to the locations then return to class in the afternoon. There they would show their works to each other and to Kiarostami. After they spoke with Kiarostami they made note of weaknesses and blind spots then utilizing Kiarostami's suggestions and guidance they would go back and edit their films. Kiarostami also made a few short films during this time and edited them with the students help so they could learn from him up close and personal. The connection between Kiarostami and his students was far more than just a regular teacher-student relationship. If you walked into the classroom for the first time you could not differentiate who was the teacher and who was the student.

They were so impatient to see the finished films and wanted to see how the stories they had listened to turned out. They had all become aware of the importance of storytelling during the filmmaking and editing process. They also learned how much the deletion of the extras, which Kiarostami emphasized so much helped them to improve and speedup their work. The class atmosphere was not like any regular school with neat chairs, tables or a teacher seated behind a desk giving basic class information. It was a workshop in its true meaning. All the films were shown on the last day and they all came out great. Kiarostami felt this was one of his best workshops to date. In his opinion it didn't matter if their films came out good or bad, the important thing was that in 10 days they proved they could do it and the class would be a new starting point for them. We were now close to the end of workshop and you could see that no one wanted to leave. They felt they were just beginning.

A few months later I went to Kiarostami's house and told him that after being in his class and due to his instruction that I will not do another film for any price until I reach an understanding with myself and a personalization of my knowledge. How could I convey my thoughts to my work if I don't have a clear understanding of my surrounding world? Now I wonder how people proceed in making films easily without this understanding. The result is a massive number of films and it made no difference.

Kiarostami told me, "This is natural because they have no other job and when you are a filmmaker that means it is your profession and you must make movies to make money. This idea of yours is good when you are relatively in comfort and have no worries about income. We cannot disregard the people who choose cinema as a profession and cannot tell them why they had done so. I think cinema is an industry to them lest art."

Kiarostami's teaching was to separate cinematic art from industrial art. An art form that one may not be able to run his life by and the ones who go after cinematic art may always stay as independent and unprofessional filmmakers. By unprofessional I mean hobbyists who do not make money from films. He believes if I expect something personal and familiar from cinema then like in any other work I must naturally evolve and gain the knowledge that belongs to what I intend to do because you cannot reach anywhere though borrowed or *dye in the wool* knowledge. You can gain any kind of knowledge these days but it is of no use if it is not yours. He really didn't think it was any problem when I said I didn't want to do any film and that the world I wanted to discover for myself may be so reachable because it needed persistence, study, self-awareness and endeavor. I will eventually reach that day and if I don't it doesn't matter. It is no problem if someone in these classes came to the conclusion about what the necessity of filmmaking is or even to say I don't want to make films any more. The important thing is to reach a correct understanding of ourselves and find our strong and weak points.

Mahmoud Reza Sani

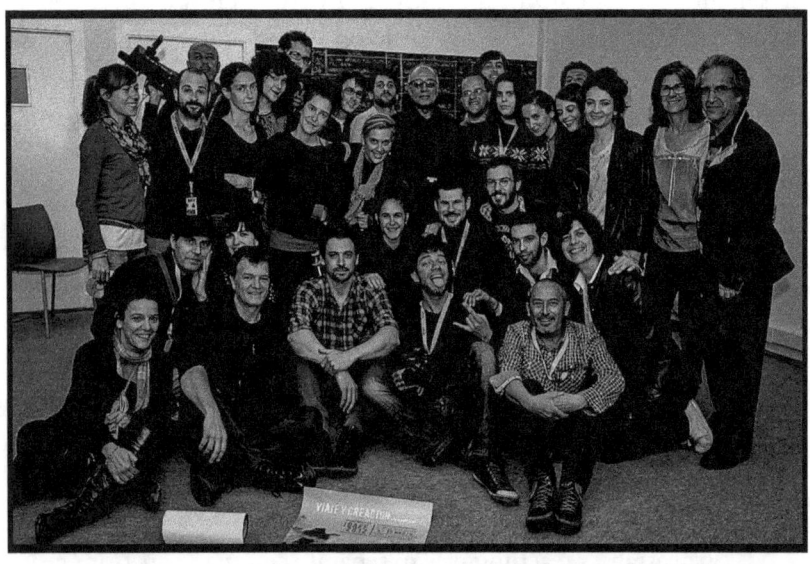

Abbas Kiarostami with the Class.

About the Author

Mahmoud Reza Sani (b. 1974 Abadan, Iran) is an award winning filmmaker and the president of the Ibn Arabi Film Festival (2010-2014) located in Murcia, Spain. He has written, directed and produced several short and feature films, documentaries and television serials.

In 2000 he founded Arvandan Film Production which specializes in low budget, high caliber documentaries and films often shot under difficult conditions.

Mahmoud is also considered the 'ambassador' of Cine Pobre, an universal movement created by the esteemed Cuban film maker Humberto Solas, an active network of international cooperation that promotes Cine Pobre (poor cinema) production by making high quality, low budget independent films. The idea which helped inspire his own company.

His debut film, "Siyamo," a poetic song of peace which tells the search for his beloved in the devastation of a post-Taliban Afghanistan won the Cesare Zavattini Grand Prize at the First International Cine Pobre Festival in Gibara, Cuba (2002). In April 2006, his film "Wild Goose," which depicts the folly of war through two opposing characters, received the special Poverty Zero Award from the NGO OIKOS, the sponsor of the film festival. In 2010 Mahmoud served on the jury for the film festival. He has also served as a jury member at Social Film Festival 2005, IBAFF film festival 2011, Carthage Film Festival in Tunisia 2012 and the Huesca International Film Festival Spain 2013.

Mahmoud holds various workshops throughout the globe to impart his knowledge and experience to those with the desire to learn and a story to tell.

About Kiarostami

Abbas Kiarostami, more than a teacher of film and a leader of creative freedom, is a fountain of wisdom and being close to this flowing stream is both a fortune and an adventure.

He was born in Tehran on June 22, 1940 and from an early age showed great fondness for images: plotting them, painting them, putting them in motion, accompanying them with sounds and silence, filling them with stories both real and fictitious, beautiful and shocking. as befitted them. He studied Fine Arts at the University of Tehran. He was a graphic designer, and subsequently created a film section at the Center for Intellectual Development of Children and Young Adults. It is there where he made his first film "The Bread and Alley," a neorealist documentary. That was soon followed by feature films such as "Where is the Friend's House?" (1987), "Close up" (1990), "Life, and Nothing More" (1992), "Through the Olive Trees" (1994) and "Willow and Wind" (1999). In 1997 he received the Palm D'Or at the Cannes Film Festival with the film "Taste of Cherry," becoming the universal exponent of a new wave of Iranian cinema. In 2010 his film "Certified Copy" received Gold in the 55 SEMINCI at Valladolid and San Francisco festivals. Juliette Binoche also won the Best Actress award at Cannes in 2010 for this film. His career in film stacks up now with over 70 awards and nominations.

Abbas Kiarostami is an emblematic figure of world cinema, especially identified with conceptual freedom of expression and aesthetics. But his creativity flies freely in other artistic genres such as poetry, photography and arts installations. Thank you, Abbas, for showing that the word life also means creation and freedom.

Mahmoud Reza Sani

www.ingramcontent.com/pod-product-compliance
Lightning Source LLC
Chambersburg PA
CBHW071553220526
45469CB00003B/1003